TEMPEST OVER EUROPE

TEMPEST OVER EUROPE

ROLAND BEAMONT

Airlife
England

Dedication

To the pilots and ground crews of the Tempest Wings of the Royal
Air Force in the final air battles of World War II over Europe.

Copyright © 1994 by Roland Beamont

First published in the UK in 1994
by Airlife Publishing Ltd

British Library Cataloguing in Publication Data
A catalogue record for this book
is available from the British Library

ISBN 1 85310 452 3

Printed in England by Livesey Ltd., Shrewsbury

Airlife Publishing Ltd.
101 Longden Road, Shrewsbury SY3 9EB, England

Contents

Author's Note

The opinions expressed in the following chapters are the author's own and do not necessarily reflect those of any other authority referred to in the text.

Acknowledgements

For their generous assistance in the preparation of this book my grateful thanks are due to: Joan Moores for her enthusiastic and exemplary typing; to the Imperial War Museum and John W.A. Taylor for their valuable help with photographs; to *Aeroplane Monthly* magazine and, as always, to my wife Pat for her dedicated, much-valued and disciplinary proof reading.

The Jacket
The jacket painting by Peter Westacott depicts a moment in the combat over the Reischwald Forest described on pages 97 to 99.

INTRODUCTION

In 1944, the year of the invasion of Normandy by the combined forces of the Allied Nations, Fighter Command of the RAF, covering the daylight hours defence of the United Kingdom, was equipped with Spitfires Mk V, IX, XII and, just coming into service the most powerful and fastest Spitfire at the time, the Mk XIV.

This range of Spitfires provided excellent capability from low level with the clipped wing V, IX and XII low-flying (LF) Marks, to the high-altitude IX and XIV, to meet the potential threat of the later series Bf-109Gs and FW-190s of the *Luftwaffe*; but there was one area of concern.

It was known that the Me-262 twin-jet fighter was in large-scale production although not yet in operational units, and that it was expected to be at least 100 mph faster than the Allies' best available fighters.

In preparation for the invasion the RAF's 2nd Tactical Air Force was equipped and ready to go with Spitfire Mk IXs for fighter cover and twenty squadrons of the, at last well developed and very effective, Typhoon heavy fighters for the ground-attack role; and also two Wings of Mustang 111 long range general purpose fighters.

For night defence and 'intruder' operations both commands were well equipped with the latest Mosquito night fighters which were much superior to any of their German counterparts.

So the stage was set for what was expected to be a great air battle for Europe, and at this late stage a new British fighter came into the scene.

In parallel to the long period of development of the Hawker Typhoons from prototype first flight in 1939 to first successful ground-attack operations in 1942–43, the Hawker company had developed the basic design into a much-improved 'Typhoon 2'. This aircraft featured an all-new thinner section (10 per cent thickness/chord ratio) wing and an up-rated Sabre engine, together with a redesigned windscreen and one-piece sliding canopy giving much improved combat vision, and also new-concept spring-tab ailerons to improve combat manoeuvrability at high speed.

In prototype trials beginning in the summer of 1943 this new fighter showed great improvement and potential to become a very effective general purpose air combat and ground-attack fighter.

The aircraft, now called the Tempest V, began to enter the squadrons in January 1944 with a higher maximum speed at low and medium levels than any other piston-engined fighter type on either side at the time, and a very much higher practical diving speed capability. It could catch anything in service in the *Luftwaffe* and, as it was soon to prove, in the dive even the Me-262 jets.

Two Tempest squadrons were complete and operationally ready by April 1944, and they patrolled the beach-head on D-Day at the beginning of an intensive and very successful period of operations. The Summer of the Tempest had begun.

Following the successful introduction, in September 1944, of No. 122 Wing's Tempests into the battle for Germany at Volkel in Holland, 2nd TAF's* most advanced

* 2nd Tactical Air Force (RAF.)

main base, with five Tempest squadrons, Nos. 3, 486, 56, 80 and 274, a second Wing, No. 135, consisting of Nos. 33 and 222 Squadrons, moved out to Gilze Rijen in December 1944. From then to VE Day approximately 150 Tempests were in continuous operations, mainly beyond the front line and over the Rhine into Germany. Their main tasks were air superiority (combat air) patrol, rail and road interdiction and, for those squadrons carrying bombs and RPs, pinpoint targets such as radars, vehicle concentrations and military headquarters, spearheading the advance of the ground forces.

With long range tanks normally carried, the emphasis for the Tempests was on penetration ahead of the main battle to disrupt the enemy's communications and supply routes, while the close support of the British and Canadian armies' land battles was covered so effectively as before by the now highly experienced and aggressive Typhoon force.

They made a formidable combination, and the Tempests with their increased speed and combat manoeuvrability were well able to take on enemy fighters themselves if intercepted during ground attack missions.

From their arrival in 2nd TAF in September 1944 to the end of hostilities in May 1945, Tempests destroyed 240 enemy aircraft (EA), and 122 Wing recorded the highest score of train attacks of all the fighter Wings in the battle.

The enemy held them in considerable respect, finding that their Bf-109s and FW-190s were no match for Tempests in speed and manoeuvrability at the low altitudes in which the final phase of the battle for Germany was fought, that is from 15,000 ft down to ground level; and any 109 or 190 pilot unwise enough to try and dive away from a Tempest was unlikely to survive.

Hans Werner Lerche, a senior test pilot at the

Luftwaffe Rechlin test centre responsible for evaluating captured Allied aircraft wrote:

> This exceptional aircraft (the Tempest V) was an improvement on the Typhoon which in performance and aerodynamics was quite stunning . . . but there was no doubt about this one; the Tempest was an impressive highly powered aeroplane by any standards . . . even faster than the P51B Mustang and only German series-production fighters fitted with the new DB603 and Jumo 213 engines could keep up with this performance.

From October 1944 the Me-262 jet began to appear in the Volkel sector but, fortunately for the Allies, it was mis-employed as a low-level fighter bomber on the controversial but direct orders of the Führer; and soon there were reports of sightings by Allied fighters which could not get anywhere near the 262s as they made shallow dive attacks at our airfields, dropping light loads of anti-personnel bombs at upwards of 500 mph.

But on 13 October Bob Cole in a Tempest of No. 3 squadron caught one in a dive at over 500 mph and shot it down near Grave.

This was the first of a number of Tempest successes against the jets and by May 1945 Tempests had destroyed fifteen and damaged eighteen 262s, more than any by the other types of fighters, including the next most successful, the Spitfire XIV.

A number of planned operations were carried out from Volkel in which Tempests patrolled the first operational Me-262 jet base at Achmer near Osnabrük about forty minutes flying from Volkel, intending to intercept 262s taking off or returning short of fuel from bombing missions.

These were hazardous operations, as the enemy set up dense flak defences round the airfield and some Tempests were lost. But there was soon a mounting number of victories, the most notable being the shooting down of 'expert' Walter Novotny, commander of the Achmer-based 262s of JG7, on 8 November 1944 by Tempests of No. 122 Wing at Volkel.

The pilots enjoyed their Tempests hugely. Here was a fighter with the power and rugged strength of the Typhoon, but with subtle differences in general 'feel' and handling qualities. It had the same rock-firm stability in pitch and yaw as the Typhoon, but was crisper and livelier in roll right up to its uniquely high Vne speed of 545 mph.

Smooth ease of control stemmed from the all push-rod operated flying controls and the new spring-tab ailerons, and quite contrary to the advice in the official Pilot's Notes (which were much criticized at the time and quite probably were inspired by a 'Spitfire' bias at the Boscombe Down Service trials centre), the Tempest was well behaved at low speed in the landing configuration and could be flown in the approach and landing pattern safely at speeds similar to the docile Typhoon. Only at the stall, static and dynamic, did it tend to drop a wing as did most other fighters of the period.

The precision of control on all axes gave it exceptional gun-aiming qualities, and its 20 mm cannon fire could be concentrated on ground and air targets with greater accuracy than most other fighters, especially in comparison with the delicate and defused spread of fire caused by the wing flexing and marginal directional damping of all marks of Spitfire.

An additional bonus for the fighter pilot was the optimized field of view from the Tempest provided by its specially developed thinned-down windscreen frame

11

structure combined with a one-piece transparent sliding canopy which gave almost unobstructed vision through 360°.

To this was added a gunsight directly reflected onto a specially graded armour glass windscreen, which provided the pilot with vision of his ground or air target unobstructed by anything but the gunsight-aiming spot and ranging graticule. This was unique in day fighters of the period, although similar systems were provided in late-model Mosquito night fighters and on some of the last RP-equipped Typhoons.

In flight the Tempest was exhilarating in a different way to the lithe delicacy of all marks of Spitfire. Its wide undercarriage eliminated undue sensitivity to crosswinds or the undulations of grass airfields, and once the power swing to the right in take-off was mastered by progressive increase in throttle combined with smooth input of left rudder, there were no further problems on that score.

With undercarriage retracted and power reduced to cruise, 300 mph IAS came up quickly, and at full throttle and fine pitch 400 mph plus could be seen on the ASI at low level with ease; faster by a considerable margin than all other fighters of the period except the jets which did not appear until the second half of 1944.

It was of course this low-level high speed coupled with accurate gun-aiming that proved so effective against the V1s.

Then the other performance characteristics. The maximum speed at MPA* variously quoted at 435–445 mph TAS and measured normally at the factory at 437 mph, compared well with most of the contemporary fighters, e.g. Spitfire IX — 407 mph; Spitfire XIV — 448; P51d — 440; P47 Thunderbolt — 425; Me-109G6 — 430; FW-190 — 416; but the Tempest's 416 mph IAS at sea level (with 150 grade

---

* MPA — maximum power altitude.

fuel) was faster than all of them at low level — for example, Spitfire XIV — 365; Mustang 111 — 375; FW190 — 350.

This edge gave the Tempest pilots a clear and confident advantage in the hard-fighting winter of 1944; and when the greatest bonus was added, the practical and fully manoeuvrable dive limit of 545 mph — at least 60 mph clear of the fastest of its competitors — the Tempest was seen to out-perform them all at low and medium altitude where it counted most.

In terms of combat manoeuvrability the heavy Tempest could be held in the turn by 109s and Spitfires up to about 350 mph, but not by 190s at any speed. Over 350 the Tempest had the edge, and above 450 where the Spitfire's and 109's controls were almost locked solid in roll and pitch, the Tempest was supreme.

All normal aerobatics were easy, but when demonstrating to VIP audiences (such as for visiting Russian generals at Newchurch on 30 August 1944 in 'RB' JN751) the author used to begin a display with a full power 45° bank left climbing turn from take-off, winging over at 1000 ft back down to 50 ft at the airfield boundary and reaching 500 mph IAS at about mid-airfield, pull up to about 70° and hold the zoom until rolling inverted at about 8000 ft.

Then, still at full throttle, putting through into a 65° dive until with the airfield again centred in the windscreen, pulling out at 50 ft along the strip at 500 plus mph; thence to pull hard up at 4–5G into a vertical upward roll and then a roll-off-the-top at 8–10,000 ft — all this before entering a low-level aerobatic pattern. It never failed to impress, and it was most enjoyable to do!

It also resulted in mounting confidence in the potential combat ability of these fine fighters, a potential which was to be fully and successfully exploited in the months to come over Europe.

13

CHAPTER 1

FIGHTER GROUND-ATTACK IN THE RAF — THE EVOLUTIONARY YEARS

W hen World War II broke out in 1939, the Allied air forces of France and Great Britain had no formal policy for the employment of fighter aircraft in the ground-attack role, and neither had the American air force, although they did not become involved in the war until 1941 after Pearl Harbor.

The fighters equipping the RAF and L'Armée de l'Air mounted only small calibre machine-guns which were barely adequate for close-in air combat and had little potential for effective use against other than 'soft' ground targets: and the British authorities were dismissive on the subject — fighter aircraft, it was said, had no effective role to play in the ground battle. Targets in the path of our ground forces would be attacked by aircraft of Bomber Command — end of discussion.

This was remarkable in view of the major effect on the land battles twenty years earlier which had been achieved by many hundreds of Sopwith Camels, SE5As and Bristol Fighters of the RFC, and SPADs and Nieuports of the French air force, when attacking the trenches and supply lines of the enemy in the final major battles of World War I.

These fighters carried two, or in some cases only one, forward-firing machine-guns, but in the hands of skilled and determined pilots their ability to seek out and pin point military targets such as troop concentrations, gun

15

batteries, machine-gun posts, supply lines and support activity, and attack them with machine-gun fire from close range, proved to be of significant importance in the closing stages of that war.

Subsequently these lessons were not forgotten in the 1920s in the Frontier wars in Jordan, Iraq and Afghanistan in which the DH9s and Bristol Fighters of the RAF were virtually decisive in subduing tribal rebellions by pin-point machine-gunning and low level bombing attacks; but by 1939 all this experience had been lost or forgotten.

The role of the RAF was now apparently to strike selected enemy targets at night with the Whitley long-range heavy bombers of Bomber Command, and by day with Blenheim twin-engined and Fairey Battle single-engined medium altitude light bombers. Fighter Command would provide air defence of the UK and air cover of our ground forces and coastal sea forces.

There was no briefing or discussion of the possible use of the Hurricanes and Spitfires tactically against ground targets, and therefore no training for this specialized activity.

By contrast, in the *Blitzkreig* of May 1940 in France and Belgium the *Luftwaffe*, equipped with Bf-109s and 110s both heavily armed with cannons and machine-guns, was directed equally against Allied air activity and against ground transport targets. At first these latter attacks were limited to military vehicles, supply transports and troop movements; but as the German Panzers' breakthrough occurred, the *Luftwaffe* made widespread attacks on all roads to the west from the Belgian and Luxemburg frontiers carrying retreating British and French forces and, very soon, thousands of refugees.

To the German high command a blocked escape route was just that, and whether it was blocked by burning Army trucks or by terrified civilians was immaterial.

In this action the 109s and 110s proved deadly with

16

the accuracy of their strafing attacks, and their contribution to the success of the lightning thrust of the Panzers to the Channel coast was very significant.

If the British authorities reacted to this it was not apparent then or until much later in the war. But in the Air Component of the British Expeditionary Force in France, Wing Headquarters gave local orders on a number of occasions, in the last few days before the inevitable evacuation, for individual pilots to strafe any 'opportunity targets' on their way back from interception sorties. Some successful attacks were made on columns of troops and supply vehicles, but these were individual and not on a large scale because of the, by then, critical shortage of our fighters.

The RAF fighter pilots surviving the battle of France returned home with the images of the strafed columns of refugees much on their minds, and there was frequent discussion of 'when shall we be put on ground-attack?'. But it did not happen then nor for some time to come as the critical Battle of Britain absorbed all the fighter capability of the RAF in the summer of 1940 until the successful conclusion at the end of the year.

In 1941 Fighter Command returned to the offensive across the Channel still in the air combat role, until the spring when some squadrons began experimental low-level operations in sections of two aircraft, generally in poor weather or (in the case of one squadron, No. 87) in pairs or single aircraft by moonlight.

These sorties were aimed at road and rail transport and 'targets of opportunity' such as troops, gun-sites, power transformers and canal barges. In fact anything likely to be part of the enemy's war effort which could usefully be attacked with multiple machine-guns.

These actions, code named 'Rhubarbs', demonstrated that fighter ground attacks against pin-point targets could be a practical and accurate method, but they confirmed that the 303-in Browning machine-guns of the Spitfires and Hurricanes were effective only against 'soft' targets, and that for the full potential of this type of operation the heavy, high velocity Hispano 20-mm cannon now beginning to appear in the new fighters would be essential.

Spitfires armed with two 20-mm cannon and four .303-in machine-guns had begun to reach squadrons in autumn 1940, but their effectiveness had been limited for some months due to unreliability of the cannon installation. By 1941 however the situation had improved, and the Hispano cannon began to show excellent results in combat over Northern France.

The first squadrons to receive the new Hurricane 2c in 1941 with four 20-mm cannons were 79 and 87, and this formidable fire power transformed the Hurricane into a potent ground-attack fighter. No 87 and other squadrons in fact used their cannon very effectively against the coastal gun defences at Dieppe during the major raid in August 1942.

Up to this point there was no established policy in the RAF for a specifically trained ground-attack fighter force, nor was there in the USAAF; whereas the *Luftwaffe*, building on their successes in Belgium and France in 1940, had developed a massive capability of dedicated ground-attack aircraft including Bf-109, FW-190, Henschel 123 and Me-110 and, from 1944 onward, by Hitler's own decree even the Me-262 jet which with its high speed and altitude combat potential was clearly misapplied in its low-attack role.

The Allies eventually came to their senses, but after a whole year (1943) of gradually increasing ground strafing activities which were only seen as secondary tasks for their fighters and fighter/dive bombers; and by early 1944 the Typhoon strike force of RAF 2nd TAF, and the P47

18

Thunderbolts and P51 Mustangs of the US 8th Air Force were trained and highly effective in the use of gun-attacks on ground targets in addition to their low-level bombing and rocket-firing roles. In this phase it was seen that the 20 mm cannon of the Typhoons was much more effective, accurate and hard-hitting than the 50-in calibre guns of the P47s and P51s, but the coming invasion of Europe was too close for anything to be done about it in time.

Following the Dunkirk evacuation and the return to these shores of the survivors of the shattered British Expeditionary Force of 1939–1940 there was, at least in the eyes of the Air Force, abundant evidence from the successes of the *Luftwaffe* in the 10–30 May 1940 campaign to show that a fighter force, suitably armed and trained in ground-attack, had great potential for the disruption of the vital road and rail links supporting any major ground operation. But the lesson was absorbed remarkably slowly in this country.

One year later by the spring of 1941 there was still no evidence in Fighter Command of plans for ground-attack training in preparation for the inevitable battles to come; and although many in the Air Force were convinced that this was now a matter of urgency, because the combat pilots in the air defence fighter squadrons could not be expected to become suddenly effective in a new specialized role without training that would also require planning, facilities and time, there was still no apparent sign of interest in high places. Then a series of unconnected incidents highlighted the problem.

In early 1941 a Hurricane squadron was briefed to carry out one of its routine and simple air-to-ground firing sorties on the Army Larkhill firing range. These sorties were normally to demonstrate machine-gun serviceability and to give the pilots periodic gun-aiming practice against 10-ft square canvas targets, and there was no emphasis on

19

tactical training; but on this occasion there was a significant difference.

The squadron commander was notified that his pilots should 'put on a good show' (of gunnery accuracy) as there would be a VIP audience! In fact this was a first sign of War Office interest, and a large group of senior army officers and Ministry officials had been notified to witness this demonstration of fighter fire-power.

The order had arisen, it was learnt subsequently, because of the mounting concern about the difficulties which Bomber Command were continuing to experience with the limitations of their equipment in achieving reliable identification of small, important targets, and then having sufficient accuracy to destroy them.

On the day conditions over the range were difficult with thick haze under a dull sky; subsequent hindsight suggested that the exercise should have been cancelled.

In fact it was not, and when the squadron arrived overhead on time, the correct 'clear to fire' signal lights were seen (there was no radio range control at that time), and the CO led his twelve Hurricanes in, each one for a single firing pass at a line of standard targets.

But in the murk and gloom he mis-identified the target, and opened fire with his eight Brownings from about 300 ft down to 150 ft at a rectangular patch on the indistinct hillside which turned out to be the spectators' enclosure!

A number of the following pilots assumed that the CO's target must be correct and fired in their turn, and it was only the tail-end of the squadron that saw 'cease fire' red warning flares come up in time to stop them firing.

This tragedy cost many lives and over one hundred casualties. The Air Officer Commanding the Group lost his command; a major review of air-to-ground firing range procedures ensued, and the cynics said 'Maybe the Army will have a different view of fighter support now'. But if they did, it was not immediately apparent.

Later that summer, when commanding a flight in No. 79 squadron equipped with Hurricane 11Cs, each fitted with four of the new 20-mm Hispano cannons, I received a 10 Group order to 'defend' the South Wales ports against a land exercise by a mobile Army force at brigade strength and protected by armoured vehicles. The 'enemy' forces were grouping in north-east Wales and I was given the timings and probable routes of their approach through the Welsh valleys.

We were based at Fairwood Common and the day dawned in normal fashion for the Gower Peninsula (where local folklore had it that, 'It'll be raining on the Gower in a quarter of an'ower!') — it was raining heavily with a low cloud base which would, I knew, be sitting firmly on the mountains on each side of the valleys we would have to fly through.

This meant map reading up one winding valley into the next and so on, with my flight hanging on to my tail grimly in the mist and rain — one error by the leader could kill them all!

But I had decided with the station intelligence officer that almost certainly the main Army thrust would be down through Pont-a-Dulais, and I calculated that if I could attack the head and tail of the column before or at the bridge in Llandeilo, with our forty-eight cannons we could, in theory, reasonably expect to stop them, possibly for some hours; and of course, once attacked they could soon be attacked again.

The fierce weather had forced us right down to the roof-tops as I recognized the town on my map, and there, right in front of us and stretching into the misty hills to the north, was a line of Army vehicles with Bren carriers in the lead.

21

In the narrow valley under low cloud there was barely room for even a simple line-astern simulated attack, but we did this twice (to rather excessively low level!) and then wound our way back through deluging rain in barely visible contact with the valley bottoms, until coming out with relief over the low ground of the Gower.

Despite my report on landing that we had most probably 'brewed up' a number of troop transports, some of them actually on the Llandeilo bridge and all in a narrow congested road with no off-road possibilities for the remainder to get by, the squadron was sent off to attack again, this time finding the column almost at the outskirts of Swansea; and my protest to 10 Group that they couldn't possibly have got that far received the response 'The Army say that fighters couldn't stop them; they had shot them all down with their two Lewis guns, and the Hurricanes had all been flying too low anyway'!

Later that day I spoke to the Army liaison officer (with the RAF for the exercise) and he also expressed the strongly held view that 'fighters couldn't possibly have stopped his chaps'!

Meanwhile practical lessons were now being learned in the Desert War in Africa and both sides began, inevitably, to use whatever was available when the going got tough. Hurricanes and 109s soon became involved in the ground battle, of necessity and with good effect.

In urgent support of this developing campaign it was seen that a fighter might be effective against armour if it could carry heavy anti-tank weapons, and a tropicalized Hurricane was developed quickly at Hawker's Langley factory to carry two 40-mm Vickers anti-tank guns.

I took part in the handling trials of this prototype installation in a Mk 11D, and the rugged, stable and forgiving Hurricane was shown to carry these heavy and

22

bulky weapons without major problems, except of course some loss of performance.

Before its final entry into service the authorities required a convincing demonstration and accordingly a trial was set up, again at Larkhill, in which a tank was to be attacked by the prototype 40-mm-gun Hurricane flown by a service pilot, who had had some brief training on the system.

On the day of the event the Army positioned a Valentine tank on the range, and then the tank commander asked the RAF exercise controller what time his tank would be released 'to take it home'. There followed a much-repeated dialogue along these lines:

RAF: 'You won't be taking the bloody thing home.'

Army: 'Oh yes I will — you'll never hit a tank with that contraption.'

About an hour later the first two rounds from the Hurricane destroyed the tank, and the tank crew needed to find alternative transport to get home.

The production version, the 40-mm-gun Hurricane Mk V, was used with considerable effect by courageous pilots at deck level in the Desert where they were able to destroy many tanks; but they were very vulnerable, of course, to concentrations of light flak that had to be avoided as far as possible or suppressed by other Hurricanes when available.

It was against this background of reluctance to appreciate the potential of the fighter aircraft to give direct support to the ground battle, that the Typhoon was eventually forced through its many development problems and setbacks to grow into the RAF's first dedicated fighter-bomber.

CHAPTER 2

TYPHOON

In 1940 the great air battles over France and England were fought with fighter aircraft with similar performance in terms of speed and combat manoeuvrability, though each aircraft had certain features which proved superior in some circumstances.

RAF Fighter Command was equipped with the Hawker Hurricane and Supermarine Spitfire which were both highly manoeuvrable and could out-turn the *Luftwaffe's* Bf-109 at all altitudes.

The 109 was faster than the Hurricane though no faster than the Spitfire, but its fuel-injected engine gave it an advantage in combat when it could keep running at full power under negative 'G'; a valuable facility not available in the Merlin engines of the British fighters; and also the 109 had heavier cannon armament.

Both sides had second-line fighters such as the Boulton and Paul Defiant and the Bf-110, neither of which had sufficient performance or combat manoeuvrability to make them competitive, and these were soon relegated to night fighting after heavy losses in the day battles.

By early 1941 the 109F and Spitfire V were emerging from their respective factories with significantly increased performance, and it was soon apparent that even their maximum speeds of around 375 mph would be exceeded significantly by the next generation of fighters which were already under test on both sides.

Taking advantage of the increased performance promised by Rolls-Royce with their rapid advance in supercharger technology, the coming Spitfire IX (and also the XII with the Griffon engine) would be 400 mph fighters, though only at high altitude; and so would be the expected 109G variant and the new FW-190 about which there was much speculation and then concern when they appeared over the Channel and scored immediate successes over the Spitfire Vs at the end of 1941.

At Hawkers the policy was different as it was recognized that though a strong, straightforward fighter (which in the event proved eminently suited to the conditions of 1940), the Hurricane's relatively thick wing would preclude further effective development in performance; and as the airframe would not stretch to take a much bigger engine, Hawkers had evolved a new series of heavy fighters based on radical new 'X' and 'H' section 24-cylinder 2000 hp engines, the Rolls-Royce Vulture and the Napier Sabre.

These prototype fighters, the Hawker Tornado with the Vulture and later a Bristol Centaurus radial, and the Typhoon with the Sabre engine, had been on test at the company factory at Langley for almost two years but the programme was in difficulties.

The first (Vulture-engined) prototype had encountered severe aerodynamic problems (excessive drag from the under rear fuselage radiator), and a near-disastrous structural failure to the rear fuselage which had earned chief test pilot Philip Lucas a George Medal for landing it back at Langley without further damage.

There were also serious development difficulties with the Vulture engine which seemed likely to be insurmountable in the tight time-scale, and so by 1941 the emphasis was changing to the Sabre-engined version.

26

This, with a revised radiator mounting under the nose which improved the aerodynamics, began to show the required high performance, and 400 mph (true) speed was exceeded from low to medium-high altitude; and, of particular importance, at its design service dive speed of 500 mph IAS (100 mph more than the Hurricane it was to replace) it was fully combat manoeuvrable. It also showed promise of good gun-aiming stability and two production versions were planned, one with the unprecedented armament of twelve .303-in Browning machine-guns, and the other with four Hispano 20-mm high velocity cannons which would give it a more powerful punch than any of the current enemy fighters.

But the Typhoon was also in technical trouble. Firstly the Napier Sabre engine became seriously unreliable with a host of different failures which resulted in a mounting number of forced landings and crashes; and then one of the Hawker senior experimental test pilots, Kenneth Seth Smith, was killed in a crash which for many months was not explained. Seth Smith had already, as project test pilot on the Typhoon, made a major contribution to its ultimate success.

This marked the beginning of a series of disasters and technical and operational shortfalls which brought the massive programme close to cancellation by the end of 1942. There were also some basic aspects of design philosophy which became much criticized.

In order to achieve operational capability of this large fighter (twice the weight and 100 mph faster than a Hurricane) to use unprepared grass or desert airfields, a thick high-lift wing section had been used, and although this had achieved its purpose with excellent take-off and landing performance, the thickness of the wing was already seen to be a block against significant further performance development, particularly at

27

altitude where the thick wing suffered early 'compress-ibility' effects.

But an even stranger problem was the initial design of the cockpit, windscreen and canopy fairing. The arrange-ment consisted of heavy metal frames, car-type entry doors, minimal transparency panels and none at all aft of the pilot's head. It was a fighter aeroplane completely blind to the rear!

Fighter pilots could not believe their eyes or the explanation given that 'the operational requirement was for a bomber-destroyer replacement for the Hurricane and the Ministry did not require rear vision'.

That this was the actual position was confirmed to the author in 1991 by Sir Robert Lickley, retired managing director of Hawkers, who added that no one in the Air Ministry had seemed at all concerned until the pilots began complaining about it! A lesson here on the vital impor-tance of three-way communication between the user, the procurement authority and the manufacturer!

In late 1941 the first Typhoons (some with slightly but not adequately improved rear vision) began to enter ser-vice with 56 squadron commanded by distinguished Battle of Britain pilot Hugh Dundas.

Six months later with two new squadrons, 266 and 609, also equipped, the technical situation had not improved and a serious accident rate had developed result-ing from engine failures and from further unexplained structural failures in which, in every case, the tail units had been found separated by up to a mile from the main wreck-age. Casualties were mounting and G/Capt Denis Gillam, Wing leader of the newly-formed Typhoon Wing at Duxford, had still not been able to declare the Typhoons operational.

By midsummer 1942 the Fighter Command Engineering Branch were showing rapidly decreasing enthusiasm for the new type, and this was echoed by low morale among the pilots in what had been, before receiving their Typhoons, three of the finest fighter squadrons.

The quality of the pilots had not changed but forced inaction while the 'Spitfire' war was still going on across the Channel, coupled with an unpleasant accident rate unconnected with the enemy and the undoubted fact that the big, ugly, cumbersome-looking Typhoon was seen as a let-down after their glamorous Spitfires, had virtually blinded these squadrons to the actual qualities of the aeroplane which had yet to be put to the real test in action against the enemy, employing its best and most effective characteristics.

But these had not been thought through at that time, and squadron training in the past six months had been limited to solo familiarization, section and squadron formation practice and some air-to-ground gunnery.

Towards the end of July 1942, with slowly improving serviceability, Gillam began three squadron 'Wing' formations from Duxford in which the author took part; first as a supernumerary flight lieutenant in 56 Squadron and, from early August, as a flight commander in 609.

It was a hot, dusty and impressive experience to thunder across Duxford's bumpy grass in all-too-close proximity to the squadron's eleven other aircraft, drawing these hot-in-the-cockpit, heavy, vibrating aircraft into close formation, and then to climb away into the glaring summer sky with the other squadrons in place on either side.

Formation drill was no problem in Typhoons with their excellent stability and crisp, responsive controls, but at our normal cruising height of 20,000 ft in the dazzling whiteness above cloud, the experienced fighter pilots amongst us could not fail to notice that the essential searching of the sky on all sides and behind was severely inhibited by the massive framework of the forward wind-screen, the canopy and 'car door' window frames, and by the almost useless perspex and metal rear canopy fairing. The idea of sweeping enemy skies virtually blinkered in this contraption had no appeal whatsoever; but that is what the Duxford Wing was preparing for and serious operations began on 29 June 1942 with a full 'Wing' formation sweep of thirty-six aircraft in the area Dunkirk-Hazebroucke-Mardyke.

This was one hour forty minutes of hot, vibrating tension with the worries of structural or engine failure dominating, as we entered enemy skies, by the ever-present difficulties of peering round the thick metal frames of windscreen and canopy for sight of enemy aircraft in the intense and dazzling sun-glare.

After much further training and gunnery practice, the next 'Wing op' occurred on 24 July in support of Bostons bombing Ostend, but there were again no sightings.

The first Typhoon night operation was carried out (by the author) on 26 July from Duxford in a one-hour patrol over Norwich against plotted enemy bomber activity, but with no sightings. The Typhoon proved straightforward to operate and easy to land by moonlight, though some modifications were needed to cockpit lighting.

Wing sweeps occurred again on 28 July (to Ostend) and 18 August (Dunkirk), both with sightings of FW-190s but no combats before the enemy evaded.

Then on 19 August in a maximum effort using West Malling as forward base, three 'Wing sweeps' were flown in support of the Dieppe Raid. The first, a diversionary sweep, was in the area of Mardyke-Cap Griz Nez and encountered flak but no EA.

The second swept from the Somme to behind the Dieppe battle. Dorniers and 190s were sighted and attacked by some of the Typhoons of 266 Squadron and there were claims for three probably destroyed but two Typhoons were lost, one to a Spitfire.

Further operations at Wing strength, sometimes with thirty-six aircraft or less depending on serviceability which continued to be poor, were carried out on 20, 26 and 27 August with no combats, although some 190s 'bounced' the Wing on the 26th over St Omer without hitting anyone and then dived away unscathed.

By now it had become clear that the heavy and combat-vision restricted Typhoon was unsuitable for the air war at 20,000 ft and above, and many engineers and some pilots were saying that it was unsuitable for any war!

Despite the efforts of Gillam and the squadron commanders (only one of whom was really enthusiastic about the aeroplane), squadron morale continued to fall and by September 1942 the majority of the pilots just wanted to get back onto Spitfires.

On Gillam's recommendation the Duxford Typhoon Wing was disbanded in October 1942 and the three squadrons moved; 56 to Matlaske in Norfolk, 609 to Biggin Hill south of London and 266 to Warmwell on the Dorset coast, to give them the opportunity to counter, with the Typhoon's high speed advantage at low altitude, the newly developing tactics of the *Luftwaffe* in extremely low-level fighter-bomber attacks on vulnerable coastal towns and cities. The 'tip and run' raids.

Very soon these Typhoon squadrons were successful and began to take a steady toll of the low-level raiders, demonstrating convincingly that they were 50–60 mph faster than the latest 109Gs and 190s 'on the deck' where most of these exciting encounters took place; and in December from Manston, Kent, and North Weald, Essex, 609 and 486 scored eleven confirmed victories, three probables and four damaged.

At Biggin Hill in November a different obstruction had

emerged for 609. It was soon made apparent that Biggin Hill was for Spitfires and that the new, ungainly ('and useless') Typhoon was regarded as 'lowering the tone of the leading Spitfire Wing'. Overtures by 609 to the Wing leader elicited the response, 'Typhoons will continue with coastal patrols and will not take part in any other Biggin Hill operations.'

Immediately responding to a direct approach from the CO of 609 (by then the author) AV-M Hugh Saunders, revered Commander of No. 11 Group, ordered 609 to move in November to Manston which was within thirty miles of the enemy coast and ideally suited to investigation of the Typhoon's capabilities in aggressive ground-attack operations. 609 were given virtual *carte blanche* for trial operations at their discretion (but authorized, of course, by 11 Group Ops Planners); the CO to report back on progress.

This was put into immediate effect and, while maintaining dawn-to-dusk Channel patrols against the 'Tip and Run Raiders', additional ground-attack sorties were begun on 17 November with a successful moonlight attack* on a train at Abbeville (PR-G, pilot CO 609), and a daylight sortie (same aircraft) on 13 December to Amiens which was aborted by a bird strike.

Soon came increasing activity with raiders and 609 Squadron destroyed six more FW-190s on 20 January 1943, and the ground-attack programme was built up rapidly from 13 December** onwards when PR-G attacked a train in daylight near Le Tréport with good results.

By April 1943 609's record (since December 1942) showed over 100 train attacks*** (25 by the CO), 22 EA destroyed, 8 probables and 13 damaged, and the 'failure

* See Appendices 1 and 2.
** See Appendix 3.
*** See Appendix 4.

32

fighter' was showing in fact a foretaste of its formidable capability as a fast, manoeuvrable, rugged and accurate ground-attack fighter and low-level interceptor.

Meanwhile it had been a surprise to learn at a specially convened meeting at Fighter Command HQ in January 1943 which I was ordered to attend, that the future of the Typhoon in the RAF was not only under review but in active danger of cancellation!

It appeared that the Command Engineering Branch headed by the CTO* Wing Commander D.O. Finlay (ex-Olympic athlete and himself a one-time Spitfire pilot) were dedicated to eliminating the Typhoon on the grounds of the, in their estimation, excessive man-hours-per-flying-hour needed to achieve and maintain the required level of serviceability in the force; but they made the mistake of going on to say that 'the pilots hated it and could not cope with it'.

While many Spitfire enthusiasts could be heard giving this view at that time, there were by now an increasing number of Typhoon pilots ready to express an opposite view based on their recent and current experiences.

There were only two representatives of this level of experience in the room full of air marshals, air commodores and group captains, S/Ldr de Soomer CO of 3 Squadron and the author, CO of 609. I gave an account of the initial successes of 609 from Manston, now being followed by No. 3 from Bradwell.

I concluded by saying baldly that far from being cancelled the Typhoons should continue to be developed at high priority for bombing and rocket-firing in order to form the main RAF fighter ground-attack force for the coming vital battles for Europe.

De Soomer supported this statement strongly, and

* Chief Technical Officer

33

after a short silence Finlay said that he did not agree with 'this over-statement by a limited number of pilots': and I said, 'Have you or anyone else in this room ever flown a Typhoon?' There followed a longer and heavier silence and finally the Commander-in-Chief closed the meeting saying 'this matter needs further review'.

De Soomer and I went back to our squadrons and stepped up our attacks over the Low Countries with increasing successes*, and no more was heard of cancelling the Typhoon programme.

Meanwhile further newly equipped Typhoon squadrons had been brought into the low-level interceptor role with 'Rhubarb' ground attacks as secondary commitments from December 1942 onwards, and these, Nos. 183, 195, 197, 198, 193 and 245 soon began to show effective results.

At Manston 609 extended its attacks through February and March on transport targets in France and Belgium by day in bad weather and by night in moonlight; and some experimental dark-night attacks were also successful when trains betrayed their presence with enough steam or glow from the fire-box.

To improve attack vision at night the squadron modified the Typhoon windscreens and gunsights as 'local mods' unauthorized by Command, and duly received strongly worded exhortations to remove them which were ignored since the modifications were proving very effective!

Then the squadron received its first aircraft fitted with bomb racks to carry 250- or 500-lb bombs, one under each wing. 609 was required to carry out trials using firstly 30° shallow-dive attacks, and then increasing the dive angle to as steep as practical.

* See Appendix 5.

34

In the prevailing atmosphere of 'war-time priority' it was not difficult to set up a trial locally in order to avoid the inevitable delays of use of one of the coastal bombing ranges; and 11 Group agreed with my suggestion that a suitable target was to be found five minutes away from Manston in the shape of a wrecked ship of about 1000 tons which was almost high and dry in the Goodwin Sands at low tide and still visible (wheel-house, funnel and masts) at high tide.

In a cloudy, blustery sky with rain showers I flew Typhoon PR-S out to the wreck, carrying a 250-lb inert (concrete-filled) bomb on each under-wing rack, and after a preliminary circuit over the wreck which was listing at about 45° and seemed intact surrounded by shallow water just covering the sand, I made a sighting run across the target ship noting that there was a light cross-wind from the west.

Allowing for this in the first run I turned the Typhoon into a 30° dive from 1200 ft at about 300 mph, lined up the wreck in the GM2 gunsight, selected the port bomb and then, at about 200 ft with the target just disappearing under the nose, pressed the release switch. A slight jolt and right wing low-trim change, and then banking left over the wreck to look for the splash of a near (or far!) miss. But no sign.

An exact repeat run with the second bomb again showed no sign — where were the bombs going? I even wondered if in fact I had imagined their releases, but on landing the racks were empty and the slip mechanisms functioning correctly.

A squadron sweep over Hardelot followed with no sightings, and then a second bombing trial sortie was carried out at dusk in the same manner as the first. The first run had just the same result. No sign of a bomb splash!

On the next run I varied the technique to represent a

typical shipping strike, running in fast at low level simulating cannon firing from about 1000 yds to suppress any flak, and then releasing the bomb at the last moment before lifting sharply to clear the ship's superstructure.

Banking over steeply to port I looked back and there, all round the bridge, was a cloud of dust and larger particles shimmering in the momentary patch of light from the setting sun. The bomb had scored a direct hit in the side of the bridge causing no water splash — and so must have all the others! The Typhoon was clearly going to make a formidable and accurate fighter-bomber.

This marked the beginning of a new phase in the Typhoon's history. In addition to 266 and 56 squadrons from the Duxford Wing, Nos. 486, 257, 193, 181, 182 and 1 squadrons, which had been equipping and training during the winter months, began coming into action along the south and east coasts in January–February with mounting successes against low-level raiders and in cross-Channel 'Rhubarbs'.

182 sqdn (S/Ldr Pugh) was the first to introduce Typhoon bombing operations together with Denis Crowley Milling's 181, and they rapidly set the standard for this valuable activity; and then the Typhoon's most formidable attack capability, eight 60-lb rocket projectiles (RPs), was introduced and brought into successful action by Johnny Baldwin's 198 Squadron. Throughout 1943, 609 continued its saga of success which included a number of major operations.

On 4 April, when returning from escorting a Whirlwind dive-bombing attack* on Abbeville marshalling yards, 609 was vectored onto an 'opportunity naval target' which sounded impressive and proved to be a force of six 'R' type minesweepers and a *Sperbrecker* flak escort just

* See Appendix 6.

leaving Boulogne for a sweep down-Channel in the gathering dusk.

In a successful attack* the twenty-eight cannons of seven aircraft of 609 sank one 'R' boat and damaged another without loss, though one Typhoon (Peter Raw) was heavily hit but still managed to land back at Manston with one entire cylinder-head missing from its Sabre engine.

Later in the year, after a continuously busy summer across the Channel, came two remarkable operations. In the first on 16 October, 609, now led by Pat Thornton Brown, set off on a mission south of Paris planned to intercept a rail movement of Field Marshal von Rundstedt. The primary object was not achieved for operational reasons — adverse weather and air combat; and in the process of fighting their way back from the Paris area the squadron shot down two Ju-88s, a Messerschmitt 110, and two 109s into the Seine!

Then on 4 December in the most dramatic Typhoon air combat victory, 609, again led by Pat Thornton Brown, together with five Typhoons of Johnny Baldwin's 198 Squadron, swept across Holland at low level and arrived at Eindhoven airfield just as a whole *Gruppe* (KG2) of Dornier 217 bombers arrived from Germany. In combats right down to runway level, 609 squadron shot down seven Dorniers and 198 four more for no losses.

One of KG2's pilots who escaped was himself shot down over London a few weeks later and said, 'I thanked my stars I was not flying that day!'

With 609 still setting the pace the Typhoon force build-up continued with rapidly increasing morale, until by January 1944 twenty squadrons were in action from main fighter stations and advanced landing grounds (ALGs) all round the south coast, and the creation of a massive,

* See Appendix 7.

formidably capable and aggressive fighter ground-attack force was nearing completion.

The exploits of the RAF's 2nd Tactical Air Force Typhoon Wings, under such inspired leaders as Charles Green, Johnny Baldwin, Mike Ingle Finch, Eric Haabjörn and the most famous of all, Denis Gillam, have been fully described elsewhere.

But historians have not always been clear in their recording of what was undoubtedly the most vital contribution of air power to the final successful outcome of the Normandy invasion in 1944.

After six weeks of slogging attrition in tank and infantry battles the Allied armies had not succeeded in breaking out of Normandy by the beginning of August, and at this critical point the enemy had massed every available tank and AFV on the left wing of the Allied front with the intention of driving General Montgomery back to the Channel.

From 8 to 20 August the RAF 2nd Tactical Air Force Typhoons caught and pinned down the massed Panzers at Mortain and Falaise, causing enormous carnage and destroying the enemy's offensive intentions entirely.

The Typhoons then set about preventing the escape of the majority of the Panzers in the Falaise Gap, while the Allied air forces attacked and destroyed the enemy's only possible escape route, the remaining bridges across the Seine.

The rout was virtually complete, and the Allied armies broke through and began their massive and successful advance in the next two months to the Rhine and the Swiss frontier.

The Typhoons had created destruction, chaos and terror among the enemy to a degree not seen before in armoured battle, and the most fervent acclamations came from the ground forces themselves.

38

In a letter from New Zealand, George Eve, a soldier with the 50th Northumbrian Division, the Green Howards, from 1940 to 1945, said:-

I remember Des Scott* firing rockets just over our heads in Normandy — they used to frighten us to death! It was marvellous for the Army not to be dive-bombed and strafed as we were in the Desert and North Africa. The RAF certainly won the Battle of Normandy. We would have been in dire straits without them.

The Typhoon, a near-failure in 1942, had become a major battle-winning success by 1944–45; and the pilots, many of whom had feared and resented the Typhoon in the early days, had come to respect and even like their rugged and victorious old war-horse with its ability to strike hard and accurately and often bring them home safely with heavy flak damage.

Many hundreds of valiant Typhoon pilots were lost from the twenty squadrons in 2nd Tactical Air Force in the intensity of the fighting for Europe, and their Commander-in-Chief Harry Broadhurst said of them: 'I suppose that flying one of these aircraft (in the battle for Europe) was the most dangerous task the Air Force has ever asked anybody to do.'

So the Typhoon squadrons of the RAF and the Royal Canadian Air Force made their glorious contribution to the final victory all the way from Normandy in 1944 to the Baltic in 1945, a contribution that almost certainly would not have been available were it not for 609 Squadron's breakthrough in the winter of 1942–43; and before that the courage and dedication of the Hawker test

* New Zealander, leading No. 123 Wing, 1944.

pilots, Philip Lucas, Ken Seth Smith and Bill Humble.

Meanwhile during 1943 the Hawker Company had developed and improved the design into firstly the Typhoon 2 and thence the Tempest series of high performance medium and low altitude fighters.

These aircraft incorporated a new, thin (10 per cent T/C ratio) semi-elliptical wing, extended forward fuselage with increased fuel tankage, up-rated engines and four-bladed propellers, and an all-new 'clear vision' windscreen and sliding canopy which was also introduced on series 2 Typhoons in late 1943.

The intention was to eliminate as far as practicable the now recognized operational disadvantages of the Typhoon and improve performance and combat capability; and with the first of the series to enter service in early 1944, the Tempest V, this target was successfully achieved.

With a maximum speed of 437 mph (T) at MPA* and a service dive limit of 545 mph IAS at which it was still fully combat-manoeuvrable, the Tempest proved generally superior to all other fighters in the low-level war over Europe, its capabilities being exceeded by the Me-262 jet (in max speed only) and by the P51B and D in long range only.

Their introduction into service began in February 1944 with very little time left to get the squadrons converted and trained to operational standard before the curtain went up on 'the Invasion' in the spring.

The summer of the Tempests was about to begin.

---

* Maximum supercharger power altitude 17,000 ft.

CHAPTER 3

THE PILOTS

There had been a feeling of elation throughout Fighter Command in the summer of 1941.

By the end of 1940 the RAF had become aware that a major victory had been won over the Channel and the south of England against the world's most aggressive air force, the German *Luftwaffe*; and now in 1941 the rest of the world was in no doubt and were constantly acclaiming the victory and victors of the Battle of Britain.

The skies of the south of England had virtually been cleared of the enemy in daylight and the Spitfire squadrons were now the aggressors in daily 'sweeps' across the Channel, challenging the 109s over their own bases. The superb Spitfire was now seen not only as a young man's delight to fly, but as the battle-winning fighter about which Adolf Galland had said in 1940 to his commander-in-chief, Hermann Goering, 'give me a Wing of Spitfires!'

Whatever the complex international war situation, as the pilots saw it they'd 'got the Huns on the run!' — which made a welcome change from the previous year. But now in September 1941 a new and ponderous shape began to be seen at some fighter bases.

It was big, bulky, extremely noisy and ugly, and could by no stretch of the imagination be compared favourably with the elegant beauty of the lovely Spitfire. This was the Hawker Typhoon, described to the first squadrons receiving it as 'a bomber-destroyer replacement for the Hurricane with a top speed of over 400 mph'!

The pilots considered it dubiously. How could a thing like that supersede the lively Hurricane, let alone their magnificent Spitfires? Would it stand a chance in combat against the new 109s and FW-190s and their experienced and aggressive pilots?

But before these questions could be answered there was a new and overriding concern. Instead of improving with gathering experience, the serviceability of the Typhoons in the first three squadrons dropped steadily until by the spring of 1942 the average availability rate was less than 25 per cent, and there was a mounting and worrying list of forced-landings and crashes due to Sabre engine failures, many of them fatal. In six months of service it had not been possible to declare the Typhoon 'operational', and now came a major blow.

A Typhoon from 257 Squadron crashed in early June killing the pilot, and the whole empennage was found intact some distance away from the main wreckage. The aircraft had been in a high-speed dive and no explanation was found of the cause of the failure.

Two weeks later while the Duxford Typhoon squadrons were finally working up to full operational category, another tail came off in a high-speed dive test from the maker's Langley factory, killing test pilot Seth Smith; then a third fatal tail failure occurred in early July to a 56 Squadron aircraft.

The pilots' morale was by now at rock-bottom. Here were they still struggling, they felt, with dangerous, uncomfortable aircraft without the exhilaration and challenge of attacking the enemy daily as did the Spitfire wings, and all apparently for nothing. When would it all end and when could they get back on to Spitfires?

Individual requests for transfer mounted but were

seldom granted, and as the autumn approached the obvious and mounting dislike of the engineering branch for the Typhoon added to the concern of the pilots even more.

But there were a few of the more experienced pilots who had begun to appreciate the better qualities and potential of this heavy, fast aeroplane.

It was certainly faster at low level than any other fighter on either side. Its wide undercarriage and good basic stability and responsive but well-damped controls gave confidence in landing in much more adverse conditions than a Spitfire could cope with; and its excellent gun-aiming and very high-speed dive capability all suggested that while its general ability as high altitude combat fighter was now known to be poor, at low level it had the potential to be a formidable interceptor and ground-attack fighter.

After the Duxford squadrons dispersed to their new coastal bases in October 1942 there was a rapid rise in confidence, and with mounting successes across the Channel in the last month of the year and in early January 1943 a remarkable change in spirits occurred.

This was aided by a great sustained effort from the squadron engineers and ground staffs who set out to show that, with technical improvements now coming through from the makers, the Typhoon could in fact be made to fly well and hard.

Success followed success, and as pilots flew out across the Channel in pairs by day, and solo by moonlight, to find and attack enemy targets at their own initiative with good results and few losses, their feelings of being stuck with a failure changed to aggressive certainty that 'their' squadron was showing how to make the Typhoon a winner.

This momentum gathered pace throughout 1943 during which the new dive bomber Typhoon force was brought into action with good effect against the rapidly

43

developing V1 flying-bomb launching site system and by the beginning of 1944, the year of the Invasion, there was no more talk of Typhoon failure.

But a new breed of fighter pilot had emerged. The traditional Spitfire 'fighter boys' were still much in evidence and in demand for their essential work of establishing and maintaining air superiority; but the 'mud-movers' of the Typhoon force and the later Tempests, had become a tough, take-on-anything group of dedicated low-attack pilots, confident in their ability to take their massive fighters through anything the enemy or the weather had to offer and to strike their targets accurately and hard with rockets, bombs, or their favourite 20-mm cannon.

Gone was any vestige of misery. They were skilled, courageous pilots, proud in the task of which they could clearly see the results every day from 'D-Day' onwards, of supporting and often saving our valiant ground forces from heavy losses in the historic drive across Europe.

Their powerful role in the final victory was positive, appreciated most strongly by our armies and continuously visible to the pilots themselves. The near failure of the Typhoon had been made into a victorious success by the efforts of the ground-attack pilots themselves.

The RAF would, it was universally thought, in future have a full understanding of and appreciation for the tactical fighter.

CHAPTER 4

NEWCHURCH DIARY. FIRST OPERATIONS — THE SUMMER OF THE TEMPESTS

In the spring of 1944 with the Allied forces massing all over the south of England for the invasion of France and the Low Countries which everyone knew must be imminent, the new Hawker Tempest Vs were still rolling only slowly off the production lines at the Langley factory.

They were wanted by 'Ding' Saunders, AOC of No. 11 Group Fighter Command, as soon as possible on an advanced airfield from which they could give fighter cover over the invasion beaches and the armoured battle to follow (Combat Air Patrol in today's parlance), and also be available for immediate defence against the imminent V1 flying-bomb threat.

In fact the invasion and the V1 attack were both expected by June at the latest, and time for getting this new fast fighter into operation was short.

In February AOC 11 Group had charged me with forming the first Wing of Tempests from three of the finest squadrons; No. 56 with their tradition as the top fighter squadron in World War I, enhanced in the Battle of Britain and, more recently, the squadron which introduced the Typhoon in 1942; No. 3, one of the most successful Typhoon ground-attack squadrons in the period 1942–43; and No. 486, an exuberant bunch of New Zealanders with a brilliant record on Typhoons and a rather casual approach (as I was soon to find out) to KRs and ACIs* and to 'Pommy Bastard' Wing leaders!

With this lot, and pole-position with our brand new Tempests for the coming activities, the summer promised to be interesting and productive and we were not disappointed. Re-equipment of the squadrons began in March with 150 Wing HQ and 486 Squadron at Castle Camps, and 3 Squadron at Bradwell Bay; but there were then insufficient Tempests for 56 Squadron who retained their Typhoons initially when the Wing was brought together at Newchurch on Dungeness on the last week of April 1944.

I had chosen Newchurch out of four available airfields for the Tempests — the others were Gatwick, Headcorn and Friston — because it was closest to France, had flat unobstructed approaches and two adequate Somerfelt Tracking runways on well-drained farm land which was unlikely to become waterlogged. Hawkinge and Lympne were also nearby as useful main bases should we need more sophisticated support on our all-tented ALG.

Throughout March in the work-up training on the Tempests I had included Squadron and Wing (two squadrons) formations from Castle Camps and Bradwell, and also armament practice camp at Ayr which had demonstrated the Tempest's excellent gun platform ability with high 20-mm cannon scores of up to 77 per cent on the 15-ft square ground targets, and equally excellent air/air results on towed banners.

Then two weeks devoted to night flying, solo, then in pairs and finally in squadron formations which put a final polish on their ability to cope with whatever might be coming, and the Tempests were ready for action.

The squadrons moved to Newchurch on 28 April and were joined by 56 Squadron's Typhoons from Acklington the next day. Soon 56 learnt that their Typhoons were to

* King's Regulations and Air Council Instructions.

be replaced by Spitfire Vs until the supply of Tempests could be resumed following production delays which had resulted from an industrial dispute at Hawker's Langley factory.

With the great Invasion battle imminent and the other Newchurch squadrons proudly vaunting their superb new Tempests, this news was a blow to 56 as was the loss within a week on promotion to Wing Commander of their CO, Gordon Sinclair, a very distinguished Battle of Britain pilot. But his replacement, Bobby Hall, took on the challenge with enthusiasm, and in the event led his Spitfire Vs over the Invasion beaches at dawn on D-Day, fifteen hours before the Tempests were allowed over!

As with most of the ALGs scattered on farm or heath land along the south coast at that time, Newchurch was a totally 'under-canvas' operation. The squadrons were dispersed on three sides of the two Somerfelt Tracking runways, with a servicing Wing established in a field a few hundred yards to the north-west together with an armament section. Personnel tent-lines and mess-tents were south of the airfield, and headquarters was set up in a farmhouse near the south-west boundary. ATC were in a tented site at the junction of the E-W and N-S runways.

All other supporting operations such as sick quarters, squadron headquarters, MT and cookhouses were in commandeered cottages or farm buildings, and some vital activities requiring specialized facilities such as parachute packing were provided by Hawkinge and Lympne RAF stations nearby.

The planning by HQ's 84 Group 2nd TAF had been excellent, and I was able to declare the Newchurch Wing operational on 7 May and carry out the first Tempest operation sorties that day (and night).

Based on the successful initial Typhoon low-level operations of 609 (WR) Squadron which I had commanded in 1942–43, I planned to give the Tempest squadrons every possible opportunity to exploit their new equipment in a wide range of actions, day and night, in the short time left before the great battle which could not be more than a few weeks away.

So with the co-operation of the 11 Group Ops planners (encouraged, I had no doubt, by the AOC himself) we began a period in which each squadron operated against the enemy either on Form Ds* issued by 11 Group or, in any 'quiet' periods, on offensive sorties planned firstly by myself and then, as we got into the swing of things, sorties at the initiative of the squadrons themselves. Most, though not all were recorded in my log book:

7th May 1944	First operational Tempest sortie. Low level recce to Rouen. Aircraft RB (Wing leader's) serial JN751. Returned u/s.
7th May	Night sortie (moonlight) JN751 'Intruder' Lens-Mons-Griznez. Long burst fired at road convoy with lights, and long goods train attacked and stopped with much steam at Guines. Close light return Flak. Full shoot. 1 hr 15 mins.
7th May	(2nd night sortie) JN751. Intruder to Evreux-Rouen. Attacked long train at Evreux. Close return fire. Much steam. Full shoot. 1 hr 20 mins.

These two sorties confirmed that the Tempest was excellent for moonlight ground attack, and that the gun-aiming was as accurate or even better than with the very accurate Typhoon. My exploding SAPI rounds had in both

* operations orders.

cases lit up the targets and shown many strikes on the engines.

The Wing (and I imagined 11 Group) were slightly puzzled at all this — 'What was the Wingco up to — weren't we supposed to be a day Wing?' But then on 11 May the more serious work began.

This time I led (in JN751) eleven Tempests of 3 Squadron in a low-level Ranger at dusk to Dieppe-Evreux-Montdidier looking for *Luftwaffe* activity around the latter two airfields. We saw nothing and encountered flak at both bases so, still looking for a target for our twelve Tempests, I brought them at tree-top level and at our cruising speed of 320 mph, down across the marshalling yards at Amiens which proved to be virtually empty!

But they were not empty of flak and as a hail of tracer shells and bullets, brilliant in the gathering dusk, swept up at us, a Tempest on my right veered up and away weaving sharply. I recognized the code letters and said over the R/T, 'Don't let a little Flak disturb you Van!' (it was the irrepressible Belgian Mony Van Lierde, still with me from our 609 squadron days) — and he came back immediately, 'Eet is alright for you — they are not shooting at you!' which wasn't strictly true, but it was good for a laugh. We shot up some very active gun posts, and my No. 2's aircraft was hit by flak but got home safely.

Diving inland over Dungeness I brought the Tempests into tight squadron formation of three 'finger-fours' with their navigation lights on in the dusk as we swept low over Newchurch and broke into echelon starboard for a well-drilled stream landing on the goose-necked flare path. The year of the Tempest had begun.

From then onwards the Wing was increasingly active. 56 Squadron's Spitfires were employed daily in Channel shipping recces down the French coast which they regarded inevitably as rather boring, and the next major

Tempest operation was on 15 May when, again in 'RB' JN751, I led eight aircraft of 3 Squadron on a low-level Ranger to Rheims, Laon and Juvincourt airfields. We saw much light flak but no targets.

Leading eight aircraft of 486 Squadron on 17 May on shipping recce, we reported a large merchant vessel in Boulogne outer harbour and came under rather too accurate 88-mm fire in the process. I resolved to remember that battery in future, but some weeks later forgot it to my embarrassment!

20th May	Leading 486 (eleven aircraft). High level sweep to Lille-Cambrai-Abbeville. Uneventful, but interesting to look down at Lille Seclin airfield which had been my base with 87 Hurricane squadron in the 'phoney war' Winter of 1939/40.
21st May	Leading (in RB JN751) four aircraft of 3 sqdn. Low level Ranger to Brussels-Le Culot-Courtrai. Near Brussels attacked a tanker and trailer with a long cylindrical object like an aircraft fuselage (later confirmed a midget submarine). Destroyed both in flames, and also attacked troops manning machine-guns. Then a motor barge set on fire and four towed barges left sinking.

On 22 May at 0300 hrs I was awakened in my tent by a despatch rider with an urgent Form D from 11 Group which I read by torchlight. From dawn a massive attack was to be made by all available fighters (USAAF as well as RAF) on road and rail targets from the Dutch Islands to

Brittany, and the Newchurch Wing was given the sector Dunkirk-Lille-Amiens-Somme Estuary (which I knew well). All rail movements and military road vehicles were legitimate targets. Tactics at Wing Leader's discretion, and the operation was to be maximum effort and continuous from first light.

This was obviously the beginning of softening up action prior to invasion, and it was just what the Newchurch Wing was waiting for!

W/Cdr 'Digger' Aitken, the Newchurch camp commandant with whom I shared a tent, was well awake by now and wanting to know what all the fuss was about. I showed him the form and said that the squadrons would need 'hay box' meals at dispersal throughout the day. He said, 'Will do' and went to sleep again. Meanwhile I telephoned the 11 Group Ops planners and told them that Newchurch would operate not in squadron formations but in separate 'finger-four' sorties, and that I would lead the first at dawn. They questioned my policy of small formations, and I said briefly that it would be simpler to control an effective search and was likely to produce the best results with the least casualties. I was confident that we had excellent section leaders who were well up to this task.

Next I phoned the Duty Intelligence Officer giving him the plan and saying that I would review all the known flak concentrations in our area with him at 0400 hrs with the squadron commanders who would then brief their squadrons; and I told him to inform all the squadron commanders including 56 who would have a standby defence role during the day.

Finally I re-awoke 'Digger' Aitken to give him the timing for any of the specialist areas such as servicing, armament, refuelling and sick bay which were not already on standby.

Then I switched off the torch and lay in the darkness

of the tent sensing the night sounds and smells of Romney Marsh. This 'agricultural' existence in farmland and almost within sound of the sea was a marked, and for me at least, a very welcome contrast to life amidst the brick and concrete of the 'permanent' RAF stations, which in so many cases nestled within the outskirts of suburbia.

With no constraints on our flying from centres of population — the nearest town was well out of range of our circuit and approach paths — we operated in a dedicated atmosphere of detachment, even isolation, from the rest of the world, which made the operational work much easier; but sometimes raised problems of morale and discipline among the troops who would have liked a 'big city' within easy reach. But that was 'Digger' Aitken's problem which he dealt with so successfully that very high morale was maintained throughout that critical summer at Newchurch, and all personnel gave of their superlative best.

There would be no more sleep that night, and I struggled out of my camp bed at 0330 just as the rumble and roar of Sabre engines beginning their warm-up running broke the silence.

I drove my service Ford V8 station wagon round the rough grass perimeter to check with the squadrons, and then to the cottage which served as Station Intelligence, 3 Squadron HQ and my (Wing Commander Flying) office.

Everything was going like clockwork, and after a few words with the I.O. and the three squadron commanders, Alan Dredge (3 Squadron), Johnny Iremonger (486 NZ Squadron) and Bobby Hall (56 Squadron), I went out onto the airfield with the first light just spreading round the rim of the eastern horizon and silhouetting the wooded slopes of the ridge of hills behind Hawkinge and Lympne.

A few words with my ground crew and the armourer who had re-checked the guns of RB, and then into the

52

comfortingly familiar cockpit; stow the map, with today's courses marked in red, in its usual place to the left of the gunsight, and check the radio frequencies and emergency courses on the card fixed to the back of my left glove.

Then up on the wing came F/Sgt Olaf Priestley of the servicing Wing, an old friend from my days with 609, to see if I needed anything else. It was always good to feel the quiet, understated warmth from the ground personnel who because of their jobs could not come with us on these occasions and felt bad about that. I told him with a grin that they looked after us too well, and that I'd bring him back a parrot!

The airfield was now visible in monochrome grey light pierced by a few flickering exhaust flames as the last warming-up engines were switched off — my watch showed 0445 and it was time to go. After a half stroke on the Kigas priming pump the warmed-up Sabre burst into a staccato, exhaust-flaming roar.

The first of the operating problems then needed dealing with. For adequate vision on the ground these powerful fighters (like the Spitfires before) had to be taxied with the sliding canopy open to enable the pilot to see ahead adequately. But if there was a strong or gusting crosswind, the swirling dust and dried grass fragments, churned up by the great four-bladed propellers, could all too easily result in gritty eyes just at the critical period of take-off; and the further down the line you were in a formation line-up the more debris there was in the air! So now, despite the still dim dawn light, I taxied out with my goggles, with their Crookes B2 filter lenses, in place to keep out the dust.

Behind me with their navigation lights on the other three Tempests swung out from dispersal. Lined up on the flare path I checked the engine and fuel gauges and set the planned time of flight on the cockpit chronometer — it would give me immediate confirmation of 'time to go home' if we got into distracting circumstances.

Take-off time minus twenty seconds. Right hand raised for the benefit of my No. 2 who was ready for formation take-off just behind my right wing tip. Then I dropped the hand on to the stick and with the pitch lever already at Full Fine moved the throttle smoothly forwards to less than full throttle to leave a margin for the No. 2's formation take-off.

Then ease the stick forwards until the tail lifts, keeping carefully straight with the rudder, again because of the formating No. 2. Ease the stick back at 75, airborne, u/c up at 85, lights green at 100, No. 2 sliding into position to starboard, begin gentle turn to port out over the coast at Hythe and throttle smoothly back to climb power. Look back over left shoulder and there are Nos. 3 and 4's navigation lights cutting the corner and closing in on the port side.

A brief R/T call to Control to confirm setting course, and then 'Harlequin aircraft, Nav lights out'. We were on our way for what promised to be an interesting operation and just up our street.

Coasting out low over the sea I kept the formation down to 200 ft at 320 mph cruising to keep below the enemy radar on this clear morning with a broken cloud sheet above at about 3000 ft, and then as the low coastline of France appeared with Mardyck ahead and the hills behind Calais and Cap Griz Nez clear to the south-west, we stayed low until 10 miles off the enemy coast before opening up smoothly to climb power after a visual signal to the others.

The climb would take us into the enemy radar cover but the cloud at 3000 ft would limit the enemy's chances of engaging with light flak over the coast. I had carefully arranged not to cross in within range of known 88-mm batteries which, with their radar prediction and proximity-fused shells, could be very accurate up to 18,000 ft and more.

Levelling over the cloud sheet at 5000 ft in the early morning sun-glare and now making a fine silhouette target against the cloud tops for any enemy fighters above, although none had been advised by Control, I called, 'Harlequin Leader. Search Formation — Go' and watched the powerful shapes of the Tempests which had been close in on either side through the cloud, move smoothly out to four spans separation.

These were skilled, experienced and aggressive fighter pilots and it was good to be leading them in this big operation.

At five minutes inland from the coast on my watch I eased the formation down into the now broken cloud sheet and we broke into the clear at about 2500 ft over the flat farmland of northern France with excellent visibility all round. Now to search for targets!

With no more R/T and increasing to our tactical penetration speed of 345 mph (IAS), the farmland and villages slipped by quickly and soon I saw a tell-tale trail of white smoke or steam. This proved to be a long goods train approaching Lens and I called, 'Target 10 o'clock low. Open out and one pass.'

My first burst of 20-mm cannon fire hit the engine which immediately 'brewed' up in a mushroom of steam. Passing over it at about 100 ft and looking back through the Tempest's magnificent canopy, I saw that we were under considerable 23-mm tracer fire from the Lens mar-shalling yards and that the other aircraft were making accu-rate attacks showing HE bursts along the length of the train which seemed to have flat cars and vehicles. I called, '2nd pass' and I led them round again with excellent results. Target No 1!

Setting course again, the others barely had time to close in to formation when I saw another trail of dark smoke near a village which the map suggested was Orchies.

Pulling the formation round in a climbing turn through 1200 ft I called on the R/T, 'I'll take this one with Blue 2 — Blue 3 and 4 hold your fire' — this to conserve ammunition.

This again was a freight train and as I began a diving turn towards it I could see a flat car at the rear. That could be a flak truck, and at that moment a string of tracer shells came from it slowly at first and then flashing by close below.

I said, 'Blue 2 take the flak wagon' as I lined up the engine and began firing at about 700 yds and 400 ft. The burst was slightly short and with the Tempest's superb gun aiming it was easy to 'walk' the final burst at close range directly into the engine which brewed up very well; and Blue 2 dealt with the flak wagon and the rest of the train. Target No 2!

I then took the formation back to 1500 ft in the direction of Lille and very soon saw activity at a marshalling yard at La Bouvrie. Circling again and keeping a check all round above for fighters, I could see that there was a long train stationary in the yard with steam up and a solitary large locomotive entering the yard from the east.

Calling Blue 2, I told him to take Blue 3 and 4 down onto the train, while I dealt with the single locomotive which was then directly below.

I rolled RB inverted and pulled through into a 45° dive which I realized was too steep for precision, but if I missed with a brief burst I could go round again.

Then quickly checking wings level and with the target steady in the gunsight I squeezed out a one-second burst. The result was spectacular as virtually every shell seemed to hit the locomotive, and subsequently the gun camera film recorded the remarkable Tempest aiming accuracy. Meanwhile the others had brewed up the other train satisfactory. Targets 3 and 4!

There had been some light flak again and I called, 'any damage?' to the others. 'Negative', they said and so regrouping we continued towards the final search area, Bethune, and finding nothing near the town set course to coast-out near Calais. But almost at once I saw a puff of white ahead on a single-track line and soon saw that it was another freight train complete with flak wagon. It seemed also to consist of tank wagons and, as it was heading west, likely to be full of fuel.

Although we had made our previous attacks with short accurate bursts to conserve ammunition, we could not have many rounds left now I thought as I called 'one pass' for this last target.

As the others spread out in starboard echelon behind for the attack, I rolled in towards the train which was now passing so close to a little hamlet that little room was left for a firing pass which would not hit the village itself.

Choosing a careful line resulted in the attack being concluded in a left-banked firing pass over some houses down to roof-top height. Once again the Tempest's aiming accuracy resulted in a good concentration of strikes on the engine and flak wagon and as I over-flew it at about 50° a flash of flame occurred below.

The others came through return fire unscathed (No. 4 silenced the flak wagon) and we could see that the target was now a real flamer. Target Number 5!

Without using R/T I rocked RB's wings for the join-up, and as the Tempests slid back into formation I increased to climb power and set course for the coast and home.

Entering the cloud cover at about 3000 ft, It took a positive effort not to relax too soon — we were still over enemy territory and as we broke into the brilliant sky above 5000 ft there was still plenty of opportunity for 109s from St Omer or 190s from Abbeville Drucat to be waiting for us — and we had little, or in my case no, ammunition left for a fight.

I called, 'Keep your eyes skinned', and then as we approached my unseen but calculated crossing-out point, I increased power smoothly and eased the nose down to take the formation out at 450 mph (IAS) until we were well clear of France.

The clouds broke around mid-channel and soon the grey-green wedge of Dungeness took shape against the deep blue of the sea, and I called the others in tight as I led them in to sweep low across Newchurch before breaking up into a left-hand circuit with the Tempests moving smoothly out at my signal into echelon starboard for their usual immaculate stream landing on the rough and undulating Somerfelt strip.

As we taxied in towards 3 Squadron dispersal, raising clouds of dust and sun-bleached grass, another section of four from 486 stormed off to keep up the momentum which was maintained all day until the last section landed in the dusk.

150 Wing had attacked more than forty trains during the day, bringing back many excellent gun-camera films of the actions, and had sustained no losses and only a few minor hits.

The next day the Wing went out again and made more successful attacks, again without loss.

So successful was this part in what turned out to be a major achievement of virtually paralysing the enemy railway system in northern France, that we were told that our two Tempest squadrons had made the highest station score of trains in all Commands and we received a signal of congratulations from the AOC 11 Group.

The following day I was called to 11 Group to report on our methods and was asked why we had operated throughout with sections of only four aircraft. I said, 'Why the question?' and they replied that some quite heavy casualties had been suffered by the Spitfire Wings while we had lost no Tempests. I said, 'How were they flying?' and the reply was 'in squadron formations of up to 12 aircraft'. 'Well then,' I said modestly, 'perhaps they should try our method next time!'

The key was flexibility; two or at the most four fighters could be manoeuvred quickly and tightly to line up on targets often identified only at the last moment, whereas with an unwieldy squadron formation this was not possible. Also a full squadron flying sedately on a steady course at low altitude presented a far easier target to the flak gunners when running in to attack, or *en route* across enemy territory.

With the mounting number of satisfactory operations behind us, 11 Group now began to use the Wing more intensively.

On 27 May I led four Tempests of 486 on a Ranger to Rheims in search of enemy aircraft without seeing any, but we attacked a *Wehrmacht* staff car and truck near Amiens setting them on fire.

After this while, coasting out over cloud, I came too close to that well-known 88-mm battery at Boulogne, and at our cruising height of 12,000 ft we were suddenly bracketed by red and black shell bursts, one of which was so close ahead that RB bounced in the shock wave to the accompaniment of a loud clang and a smell of cordite — a definite hit!

This had disturbed our small formation and as they steadied I called, 'Anyone hit?' But they didn't think so, and as RB seemed to be continuing unharmed I didn't mention mine.

On landing we found shrapnel holes in RB's starboard engine cowling and wing root, but nothing that would take long to repair.

Airfield attack

The next day 28 May, was a long hot one at dispersal with no activity until, at about 1700 hrs and 11 Group ops phone rang giving an immediate 'Scramble one squadron to Cormeille-en-Vexin airfield at Pontoise, north of Paris. Target, reinforcement of twin-engined bombers within the last two hours'. The voice said it was urgent and that the movement was expected to result in a raid that night.

I called Alan Dredge, 'Scramble all available 3 Squadron aircraft. I'll lead. Target, aircraft on Pontoise. No briefing, I'll give you the gen when we get there!' The IO thrust a note of the flak defences at me as I ran out, and within five minutes the seven 3 Squadron Tempests were lining up behind for take-off.

If this hot, clear sky persisted over the other side I would be able to attack out of the late afternoon sun, which would mean running in from the west.

As soon as I could after take-off, as we streamed out over Hythe in open formation in the climb I checked the possibilities on the map. Yes, further to the west a pro-nounced bend in the Seine would make a good, positive turn-in point for our dive from 10,000 ft. All I had to do was to identify the target in good time!

These thoughts were disrupted by Alan Dredge call-ing that his aircraft had gone u/s and he was returning. He banked away with his No. 2, the standard procedure.

That left five aircraft for the attack, which was a pity as none of these could be spared for anti-flak. We would have to do the best we could.

60

With clear skies the Somme estuary soon took shape in the haze on the port side and I was able to confirm our track as we crossed the coast. Then another check as we passed to the west of Beauvais Tille airfield. Radar control confirmed, 'No trade for you', and then the last critical five minutes of the run-in until with one minute to go I still couldn't see it; but there was the bend in the Seine straight ahead.

Just at this point and some miles away off my port wing tip, there were the runways of an airfield; and in a few more seconds I could see a long white dispersal road on the west side with blast pens and then, there they were!

In four or more pens silhouetted against the white concrete were the black shapes of twin-engined aircraft!

I called, 'Target to port. Aircraft in dispersal pens down road on west side. Echelon starboard for attack, Go. One pass and make this good.'

I rolled down into a 30° dive and increased power. This was a well-defended target and we would use the Tempest's formidable gun-aiming accuracy in a fast pass.

With the ASI at 470 mph and increasing, I ruddered the gunsight on to the left aircraft in the line which was now coming fast into range. It looked like a Ju-88 as I opened fire at about 800 yds and saw the shells group exactly on and round the target. Keeping firing all the way in and correcting nose down for less bullet-drop as the range reduced the 88 was smothered in bursts, and then at the last moment as I pulled out sharply over the top a large piece flew off it and, it seemed, over my port wing. Luckily it didn't hit! Here was this splendid gun-aiming stability again!

Now down across the runways at about 480 with shell bursts and tracer fire overhead and to one side; and then we were clearing over a village with a church steeple and, looking back, there through an impressive cloud of smoke came the other Tempests weaving and jinking to avoid the flak.

I kept low for a few miles and then, rocking wings, climbing away on course for home. Behind in the target area smoke could still be seen for some time.

With the Tempests back in formation I called radar control for any activity, and they said, 'Sorry, no trade. How did it go?' and I confirmed that we had had a 'good Prang'! None of the Tempests had been hit and we had brought back some good combat film of the results.

Next day 11 Group said that a PR Spitfire had confirmed that four late model Ju-188s were still on Pontoise, destroyed or damaged,* in the west dispersal area; so this had been another successful event and had added to our growing enthusiasm for and confidence in our Tempests which had made their point, but it was some months before this particular message (i.e. small formations for ground attack) became general policy.

The next day produced another interesting operation to 'sweep' the area of Lille-Seclin-St Omer with two squadrons in the hope of finding fighters up from those bases. But they did not react and on the return leg we were diverted to Thorney Island, I think as an exercise in flexibility of the control of fighters in the last few days prior to the great adventure. We flew back to Newchurch after a good lunch at Thorney.

By now the work-up period of the Newchurch Tempests was complete and it was clear that 11 Group had come to regard us as ready for anything. Even so their level of confidence in us was to be a surprise on D-Day, 6 June!

* See Appendix 8

62

CHAPTER 5

TEMPESTS OVER THE NORMANDY INVASION

After I had attended a fascinating briefing of all the Wing leaders at Tangmere on 3 June the Wing had been stood down for twenty-four hours to obtain maximum serviceability, and during this period all aircraft were to be painted with black and white stripes on rear fuselage and both wings, top and bottom — the Invasion identity markings!

But Operation Overlord was delayed by bad weather for twenty-four hours, and then the signal 'Overlord effective 0100 hrs 6 June' was received at Newchurch as in all the other fighter units from Cornwall to the Wash.

The whole Wing was at Readiness from 0345 hrs, and as the Tempests were not warned for an early show much consumption of bacon and eggs was going on at the dispersals, although a few pilots understandably did not feel hungry and their share was accepted with enthusiasm by those with more resilient constitutions.

Bobby Hall's Spitfires got away first with a weather recce to the British sector beachhead before dawn, and later with a squadron strength 'fighter cover' of the shipping and 'Mulberry' harbour at about 0800 hrs. The Tempest squadrons became frustrated by waiting until at mid-morning I was able to lead off 486 Squadron for a convoy escort down Channel for one and a half hours during which the sea in all directions seemed to be covered in shipping of all sizes and shapes, all heading south from the Isle of Wight towards the Normandy beaches.

The Tempests maintained these patrols at squadron strength with no action for the remainder of the day until, at around 2200 hrs when I was expecting to stand-down until dawn on the 7th, we received an ops order for 'immediate Wing scramble of 3 and 486 to the British sector Ouistreham-Caen, 10,000 ft. Enemy aircraft active'.

It was almost dusk in light rain under an approaching warm front, and I lifted the '11 Group Ops' phone — this was going to be a full-night, bad weather recovery — did they really mean it? Yes, they did!

So within a very few minutes I was in JN751 leading out the line of Tempests with their navigation lights on in the murk and drizzle and, with no briefing, turned onto the flare path and breaking radar silence said, 'Harlequin aircraft line-astern climb in sections (two aircraft) to cloud tops and re-form. I will cruise-climb. Anyone who loses contact return to base. Climb on heading 220°.'

Then we were thundering down the bumpy Somerfelt between the goose-neck flares and lifting off into what was now clearly very unsuitable weather for a two-squadron formation! There was just time to settle on heading in the climb with my No. 2 tight in to starboard, when the cloud base absorbed us at about 1200 ft and our navigation lights glowed brightly in the mist and rain.

I was glad that the visibility was still adequate to see the other Tempest at about two spans and, briefly looking back, I could see the lights of the next section climbing behind. So far so good, but how were we going to get back from this crazy sortie without radar or any homing aids other than QDMs* — VDF** let-down and approaches had not been invented nor of course had PAR*** at that time.

* precision approach radar.
** radio homing bearing.
*** radio direction finding.

But that could wait and my priorities were to get this lot together and to the Beachhead in very short order. But with my rudimentary knowledge at that time of meteorology I was already feeling that a clearance behind the front might allow us in to Tangmere or somewhere further west. Meantime it was a good thing that we were all familiar with night formation in our Tempests!

With its accustomed suddenness, which was still always a surprise, the swirling cloud broke above and then we were through into the clear after-sunset sky with the north-western horizon outlined in pale blues and pinks, and the sky to the south ahead of us very dark with the first stars glittering.

I looked back and there on both sides came the Tempests drawing into good formation — they were tremendous chaps. I learned subsequently that we had ten with us and that the other five had lost contact and returned safely to base.

Meanwhile after half an hour the cloud sheet dispersed ahead and soon the flickering flashes of continuous gunfire showed clearly where the battle of Normandy was raging.

It was now quite dark and as I turned the formation towards the west directly over the gunfire flashes of battle, a mass of lights appeared ahead before I could evade them and as they rushed past overhead I saw the silhouettes of P47s. With our navigation lights out they had not even seen us, and radar had given us no warning of them.

This was getting ridiculous, and I called radar control for confirmation of our patrol as I now felt that this was a night-fighter job. They replied that the enemy activity had now died down and we were indeed being relieved by night fighters. Newchurch was now 'clamped' and we were to divert to Ford on a heading of $320°$.

I had never landed a formation at Ford or even seen it

at night, but there was a first time for everything so I told
the Wing to keep a sharp look-out and to switch on navigation lights (the risk of interception by enemy night
fighters being far less than that of collision as our
Tempests' cruising speed was well above the maximum of
the Me-110 and Ju-88 night fighters).

It was to say the least unusual to be leading a large
formation of the fastest fighters through the night sky as I
settled down over the cloud sheet again on the northerly
heading, and I began to have time to consider the next
phase of this odd operation. With about thirty minutes to
go to the south coast there was ample time to plan our
arrival at a strange base.

If the weather had cleared behind the front the
squadrons would be put to 'line astern' and then 'aircraft
line astern' for a stream joining of the downwind leg at
Ford, and the turn-in following the curved 'Drem' lighting
system to Finals on the approach lights and then the flare
path. We had practised this well at Bradwell and could set
it up with confidence.

But if the weather was IFR* this would mean orbiting
above cloud and sending individual aircraft down into the
weather under Ford's radar control for the new GCA
approaches to the runway —and this we had had no
opportunity to practise!

Meantime there was no point in worrying and it was
almost pleasurable to look round from the dimly red-lit
cockpit of my faithful RB at the mass of lights rising and
falling gently on either side and behind.

But at about twenty miles from the coast Ford ATC
came in with, 'Weather 20 miles, $\frac{3}{10}$ths at 4000'. Wind 275
at 15 mph. You are No. 3 formation to land behind two
Spitfire squadrons [whose lights I could now see circling

---

* Instrument flight rules.

ahead]. Join left-hand circuit at 5000 ft and wait instructions.'

I acknowledged with relief and then looked at the fuel
gauges. I was safe for thirty minutes, but what of the
others? I called them to confirm if anyone could not make
thirty minutes but no one responded, so on we went in
the night sky at close on midnight and soon were turning
gently left round the circle of 'Drem' lights we could now
see below, all leading to the parallel runway lights now
fully on regardless of any possible enemy 'Intruder'
activity. Then I realized another complication — clusters
of lights were also coming from the opposite direction
and circulating away on our starboard — the Tangmere
circuit was also very active, 5 miles to the west!

Although the Ford ATC voice had been calm and
unconcerned as is customary in this country, it was becoming apparent that they were under great pressure down
below, and when we finally reached the bottom of the stack
and were called in for our stream landing the final approach
was almost confusing with the hundreds of navigation
lights still apparently taxying all over the airfield ahead!

All the Tempests landed safely except one who, as I
discovered subsequently at Air Traffic Control, overshot
Ford and landed at the first flare path he saw which turned
out to be Dunsfold; and over two hundred day fighters
were landed safely at Ford that night.

So the Tempests had patrolled the beachhead on D-
Day, but it was not until D-Day plus 2 that we fired our guns
again.

7 June

On the day following the D-Day landings in Normandy, the
Tempest Wing patrolled the left flank of the battle in the
area Le Havre-Lisieux-Caen but without excitement until,
as we coasted out over the Seine bay on our way home, the

67

Beachhead Patrol Wing of Spitfires turned in to attack and opened fire at aircraft at the rear of my formation. I called, 'Opening up — watch those silly buggers at 2 o'clock' — and we drew quickly away from the Spitfire IXs leaving their leader still more worried about his inadequate aircraft recognition!

Tempests against the 109s

Then on 8 June came what we had been waiting for. At midday I led 3 and 486's Tempests to the Rouen-Lisieux patrol line again in brilliant sunny weather with broken cotton-wool cumulus below our cruising level of about 12,000 ft.

It all seemed peaceful and routine but infinitely pleasurable as I looked round at the twenty-two Tempests in steady search formation — what would this sortie bring us?

The R/T broke silence as I pin-pointed our position through a gap in the clouds. We were on track a few miles off Dieppe when Blackgang radar (Isle of Wight) said, 'Harlequin Leader, have probable trade for you. Six-Plus unidentified at 20 miles north of Rouen, no height at present.' I acknowledged and called, 'Harlequin leader, opening up.'

Increasing to maximum cruise, which gave us about 400 mph (true) at this height, I began to concentrate on the area directly ahead.

The Seine appeared curving round Le Havre to starboard as the broken cloud thinned out inland, and then Blackgang: 'Trade now 10 miles at 12 o'clock at 8–10,000 ft, probably Bandits.'

Increasing to nearly full throttle and easing into a shallow dive for tactical advantage, I called, 'Keep your eyes skinned and stay together.' The Wing was now thundering towards the northern outskirts of Rouen when I saw them — an untidy line astern of single-engine fighters crossing our heading from right to left about two miles ahead and 2000 ft below. It was a perfect radar intercept by the Blackgang controllers.

Calling Johnny Iremonger's 486 New Zealanders to stay up and cover, I took 3 Squadron round in an easy curve over the oncoming formation until we were directly above and up-sun of them, and then winged over down at them saying, 'Hold your fire, they look like Mustangs.'

Then as the range closed quickly with our good speed advantage, the gaggle ahead rolled left and I could see the slim tapered wings and rounded tips — 109s!

I called, 'Tally-ho! They're 109s — come on in,' and without need for any more power I slid RB down to close rapidly in behind the last of the formation.

At about 500 yds they saw us coming and broke very sharply to port with maximum boost exhaust smoke and curling white vortices streaming from their wing tips. Eliminating consideration of the leader and the rest, I fastened on to my target and pulled tightly inside his turn to open fire with a short burst at about 400 yds. We were closing very fast and as he rocked his wings in violent changes of bank I had to throttle back sharply to stabilize below his tail-wheel at about 100 yds, and in an over-the-vertical bank and at about 'one ring' deflection which gave an aim-off line well forward of his spinner, a second short burst showed strikes on fuselage and wing roots and he suddenly streamed smoke and oil on to my windscreen.

Breaking right as he slowed sharply, I rolled back alongside his tailplane and saw fire streaming from the wing roots but no sign of the pilot in the cockpit.

Confident of cover by my No. 2, Lefty Witman I had not looked back for a significant few seconds, and then bang! The Tempest shook, there was a strong smell of cordite and a cauliflower-sized hole had appeared in my starboard wing!

Whatever did that must still be behind so I pulled sharply up into a starboard zoom climb with full throttle, aiming for the scattered cumulus layer that was now above us as we had come down to around 4000 ft in the combat.

In the steep spiral climb I looked back but could see nothing except a trail of black smoke curving down towards a bend in the Seine. Then I was in cloud and after checking that the instruments and controls seemed normal, I called Johnny Iremonger to re-form the Wing and continue the patrol while I returned to base, damaged.

My No. 2 was not in contact but he called in confirming my 'flamer' and one of his own, and there was a confused chatter from excited 3 Squadron pilots claiming victories until I told them to shut up and re-form on 486 over Rouen.

Now to attend to my problem. The shell that had hit my right wing could have ruptured the fuel system and the undercarriage and brakes among other things.

There were twenty miles of enemy skies to the coast and 120 miles of Channel to cross to reach base; so first to set up economical cruise in and out of the $\frac{5}{10}$ths cloud cover and then to check for any signs of fuel, oil or coolant loss. Everything looked normal, but the cruise speed was well down due obviously to damage which I imagined could include a protruding starboard undercarriage, although there was no red light.

Control came in at intervals with comforting steers and assurances that ASR* was 'laid on', and then we just had to sit out the half hour crossing to the nearest point on the home coast, Hastings.

* Air-sea rescue.

70

With this eventually in sight I turned gently down along the coast on direct heading for Newchurch, and arriving in the circuit flew low past the ATC tents near the runway. They confirmed a 'bulge' under the starboard wing but the u/c apparently up, so pulling up to 1000 ft I slowed RB to 100 mph to give favourable conditions for the u/c, and selected Down. Reassuring lurches seemed normal and then green lights, and ATC confirmed 'both down' as I flew past again.

There was still the possibility of a collapse of the starboard leg on touchdown which could be unpleasant on the rough Somerfelt strip, so I lowered flaps and set up a careful and slow approach.

RB touched gently and I braced for the starboard wing to go down which would lead to a violent swing and possible roll-over onto its back, but nothing happened and as I turned directly back to 3 Squadron dispersal and opened the canopy, the farmland air, hot in the sunshine, smelled good even with its acrid mix of gusting exhaust smoke.

At dispersal the word had got round — 109s and the Wingco had got the first! When Johnny Iremonger brought in the rest it seemed that we had destroyed three, possibly four, Me-109G6s for no loss, but one Tempest (F/Sgt Rose) had had a runaway propeller and had force-landed, it was hoped, somewhere in the Beachhead area. This was confirmed later and he was returned to Newchurch by the Navy the next day!

Olaf Priestley reported that RB had received a cannon shell from above between the main and rear spars of the starboard wing, and that it had just missed the starboard fuel tank and had caused the starboard undercarriage fairing to bulge, but no further damage. The whole wing could be replaced by the Servicing Wing and in the meantime I would fly another 3 Squadron aircraft. Bob Moore had claimed two 109s and Lefty a probable, and the performance, manoeuvrability and gun-aiming accuracy of our aircraft had all proved, just as we expected, to be superior in action against the 109s*.

The Tempests had arrived and now we were in business!

* See Appendix 9.

CHAPTER 6

TEMPESTS AGAINST THE FLYING-BOMBS AND THE AIR BATTLE FOR EUROPE

I had test flown RB again with its new wing on the 13th, and further Beachhead patrols were flown on 10, 12 and 14 June encountering much flak but no EA; and then on the night of 14 June the 'Diver Alert'* was received and things like very loud motor bikes with bright orange flames tore across the night sky of Kent and Sussex for a few hours. The V1 flying-bombs had arrived!

Next day the Tempests were held at Readiness for an attack which did not come, and 56 Squadron continued their weather recce and convoy escort sorties with their Spitfires which, though valuable, were by now causing them much frustration while they still awaited their longed-for Tempests.

But on the night of 16 June the V1 attack began in earnest, and just before dawn one was shot down by a Mosquito night-fighter from West Malling.

The first in daylight fell just after daybreak to the author and Bob Cole of 3 Squadron after a short, accurate radar intercept in broken cloud and rain off Folkestone. We each fired bursts at this very small, fast target and it went down and exploded near Ashford.

What followed was a unique exercise which involved maximum utilization of all serviceability twenty-four hours

---

* Code for the expected flying-bomb attack.

a day for a long period. The operations were continuous in pairs throughout daylight hours and by single aircraft at night, and pilots were soon averaging four and five sorties of 20–25 minutes, mostly at full throttle, per 24 hours. Most sorties resulted in intercepts, and with gunnery skill improving markedly with this continual practice, pilots were often destroying two or more V1s in one sortie and sometimes as many as four.

It was arduous work and there were mounting casualties from V1s exploding under attack and also from anti-aircraft gunfire, for it soon became clear that neither a gunner firing at a flying-bomb nor a fighter pilot attacking it was going to give way to the other!

This situation became so tense for a time that some pilots threatened to strafe the anti-aircraft gun-sites that fired at them, and questions were asked in Parliament. Drastic measures were taken by both Services and the problem was solved eventually by separating the defences into 'Gun Zones' and 'Fighter Zones', but not before a number of fighter pilots had been killed or wounded.

Another feature of the period was that under such intense pressures aircraft and pilots were stretched beyond normal limits, and there were many crash-landings caused by over-stressed engines failing; and in some cases by pilot error resulting from fatigue.

Examples were Seymour 'Buck' Feldman, an exuberant American in No. 3 Squadron who, with a dying engine just failed to make it back to Newchurch and crash-landed alongside the Hythe canal. He was not injured and went on to become a high scorer against the V1s and was decorated by King George VI with the DFC at a field investiture.

In another incident Jim Sheddon of 486 Squadron, when firing at a flying-bomb flew into the spent 20-mm shell cases of his section-leader who was already attacking the V1. The No. 2 should not have been firing at all! His

Tempest engine was damaged and he crash-landed, ending up in hospital.

The mishap was a break-down in flying discipline probably resulting from stress which could so easily have had a fatal result.

In the fifty years that have passed since the end of the main V1 battles much has been written and published on the subject, some well-researched, some clearly biased and inaccurate and some distinctly imaginary!

Most have been misleading to some extent, in particular many Spitfire pilots have claimed that 'theirs' was the highest scoring squadron, and also P51b Mustang pilots (the gallant and ever-aggressive Poles) have published similar claims. The records however are conclusive:

During the '80 critical days' of the battle from 16 June the scores by aircraft types were (averaged and rounded down where discrepancies occur in the records):

Tempests
Newchurch Wing
3, 486 and 56 Squadrons: 638

Manston Wing
NFDU/501 Squadron: 88*
274 Squadron: 15

Spitfire XIV
303 and 91 Squadrons: 322

Mustang P51b
Polish Wing: 232

---

* Of the special night-flying units' total of 88, no less than 60 were destroyed by 501's talented CO Joe Berry.

Mosquito
25, 68, 85, 91, 125, 157, 219,
409, 418 Squadrons (at varying
periods and mainly at night):   428

Meteor
616 Squadron: 13

Plus 158 destroyed by miscellaneous
'free-lancing' Typhoons and Spitfires
Mks V, IX and XII and American P47s.

Total destroyed by fighters: 1744
Total destroyed by AA guns: 1460

This level of activity was sustained for over eight weeks until the massed guns of AA Command, reorganized in a narrow coastal belt and re-equipped with radar directors and proximity-fused (VT) shells, were able to take over the main defence task from mid-August onwards with greatly improved effectiveness.

During that first two months of the V1 battle the Tempests of the Newchurch Wing destroyed 638 V1s — over a third of all V1s destroyed by fighters and more than all the other defences put together in the period.

The high success rate was only made possible by the intensive and dedicated efforts of all the servicing and support personnel at Newchurch, who worked miracles to keep the Tempests flying in more arduous and demanding conditions than could have been foreseen or planned for.

During the battle 56 Squadron began to receive its new Tempests in early July and made two pilots 'operational' after only two days' training with each delivery, until Bobby Hall had his full squadron wading in and destroying their share of V1s by 8 July. He did this without accidental losses which might well have occurred under such pressure, so that by the beginning of August 150 Wing was in full fighting order with three Tempest squadrons up to strength at last.

Meanwhile I had kept pressure on 11 Group to release us back to our air superiority and ground-attack roles just as soon as it was practical to do so, and on 15 August we began our return to the battle for Europe.

With our V1 intercepts still happening every day, we returned to the offensive when I led 56 Squadron on an uneventful sweep to the Paris area on 15 August, and then another with 486 Squadron to Paris-Creil where we received some accurate flak.

Another sweep to Paris was uneventful on the 16th, and then on the 26th with 486 I found a convoy of AFVs near St Omer and attacked with good results; JN751 was hit by return fire in the cowling and wing.

Tempests against a radar target

Soon after D-Day I had been warned to plan a 'set piece' strike against one of the chain of enemy radar stations in northern France with the date to be co-ordinated with the Allies breaking out from Normandy and moving towards Belgium and the German frontier; and the order for this action came on a Form D on 28 August.

The target was a large 'Freya' radar aerial array at the village of Cassel midway between Dunkirk and Lille. It was sited on a ridge above the otherwise flat farmland of that area, and I reckoned from the Intelligence map and some good PR photographs that a low approach would reveal the very large circular radar dish in silhouette as a clearly defined target. It was mounted on the roof of a building right in the middle of the village however, and it would be difficult to avoid the risk of civilian casualties and damage.

I planned to take two squadrons for this important attack in contrast to our normal policy of small, flexible formations, as this was a fixed objective and the ninety-six cannons of twenty-four Tempests could be expected to do heavy damage to this pin-point target.

The morning of the 28th dawned clear with forecast cloudless skies over northern France, and at first light I led off two full squadrons down the flare path, Bobby Hall's 56 Squadron and Johnny Iremonger's 486, aiming to reach the target with a bright sunrise hopefully on the south-eastern horizon so that we could make our attack out of the sun.

Over the French coast the weather was perfect and I could already see the general target area twenty miles ahead. Conscious that we were tracking close to the fighter base of St Omer I scanned the sky all round intently, but with nothing seen and no radar reports of activity I concentrated on the vital map-reading of the run-in.

On time the land-marks came in to view — a railway line leading from Dunkirk towards Cassel, then a wood with a lake and then a darker line of a tree-clad ridge crossing our heading; and finally down to port just where it was supposed to be, a village crowded on the slopes of the ridge. I could see a church spire from our 10,000 ft but where was the 'Freya'? The next few minutes were critical for if I could not identify the target immediately we would have to fly round again at lower altitude until picking it up and this would alert any defences and lose our advantage of surprise.

Holding to the plan I continued past the south-west of the ridge and at about 5 miles on called, 'Harlequin leader going down to port, aircraft echelon starboard for attack, Go.'

Holding power steady at cruise rpm the speed rose

rapidly as I rolled into the dive straight out of the eye of the sunrise as I had planned with the twenty-three Tempests spreading out behind, and as we went through 500 ft at about 430 mph I saw it — high above the roof-tops ahead and the dominating feature for miles around, the unmistakable circular aerial structure of the 'Freya'.

I called, 'Target straight ahead, get down low and don't fire till your next ahead is clear'; then as tracer fire started to come up on the starboard side, 'Johnny, [Iremonger] take that flak post out.'

Sections in each squadron had been briefed for 'antiflak' if the situation demanded and they knew what to do, and then we were coming into firing position. Racing across fields at about 200 ft above ground the village of Cassel sloped up ahead to the top of the ridge, and above it all at just about my level and for all the world like a great dart-board was the Freya — a perfect target. I was not conscious of return fire although some was seen by the following Tempests, and then with easy precision RB's gunsight was ruddered on to the centre of the Freya.

Opening fire at about 700 yds I continued the long burst of 250 rounds right into point-blank and, with flashing hits all over it, and lifting at the last moment just over the top, thought, 'Christ I'm going to collect all that debris' because the hundreds of flashing HE strikes which had showed all over the aerial and into the main control building beneath it had thrown up a cloud of smoke, dust and presumably harder material.

But we flew clear, and according to plan I pushed RB down the northern side of the tree-capped ridge and levelled out at 200 ft over fields and farms for a few miles rocking my wings for the re-join, while the Tempests came through all the smoke and commotion behind. The target looked well and truly hit.

At five miles I called 'climbing' and the squadrons

were soon sliding back into Wing formation, and then we apparently came within range of a good 88-mm battery and were immediately boxed by the black puffs of accurate fire for some anxious moments.

I called, 'Anyone hit?' and Bobby confirmed that all his were OK, but Johnny said, 'One hit but seems OK'.

Keeping a close look-out for EA I called radar control for any activity and they said, 'Sorry, no trade' and I set course over the enemy coast for Dungeness, still with the sunrise streaking long dark shadows from trees and high buildings below.

It had been a classic attack with effective results and only one minor hit to a 486 Tempest; and all the pilots had had the satisfaction of long firing passes with clearly visible results on an important target.

I learned later that that radar station was still out of action when it was overrun and captured by our ground forces one week later.

Tempests over Holland and Germany

In the last week of August the Wing was finally relieved from 'Diver' patrols (I had shot down my 30th and last V1 on 23 August near Sevenoaks) and the squadrons were now in offensive action on most days. Some of these were at Wing strength and I led an 'armed reconnaissance' to Courtrai in search of the newest V weapon threat, the V2 supersonic rocket, on 1 September. We found nothing at the suspect site, but encountered some accurate light flak from Menin on the way in.

On 6 September flying a new 'series 2' Tempest V with long-range tanks (SA-H of 486 Squadron), I led twenty-four aircraft of 56 and 486 Squadrons to escort 130 Lancasters bombing Emden. Routed via Schipol and Soesterburg, we jettisoned the empty drop tanks on sighting the mass bomber stream at 18,000 ft north of the Zuider Zee and stayed with them for twenty minutes until our fuel state demanded our return. The bombers received dense and accurate flak from Emden. No EA seen. 600 miles, 1 hr 58 mins.

Then on 10 September with sixteen aircraft of 486 and 3 Squadrons another 'Armed recce' in search of V2 rockets to the Hague-Schagen area. No V2s found but a train attacked and set on fire at Schagen, and 3 Squadron attacked some barges on a canal. One Tempest of 3 Squadron ditched off the Hook of Holland, W/O Orwin, POW.

An active sortie occurred next day, 11 September, when leading (with my new RP-B with long-range tanks) sixteen aircraft of 3 and 56 on V2 reconnaissance to Den Helder. We took off from Newchurch in the darkness before dawn under a starlit sky in the hope of seeing the flame of a launching V2 in the early dawn. As we approached over a leaden grey North Sea there was ground mist throughout the Dutch islands, but the smoke of many trains showed clearly through the mist layer and after a fruitless search for V2s I decided to go for transport.

Taking 56 Squadron down on the indistinct island of Maarsluis, we quickly put a train in spectacular fire, and then another a few miles away. Meanwhile 3 Squadron attacked two more through the ground mist on neighbouring Schouen island.

We encountered some machine-gun tracer fire from the trains, and heavy 88-mm fire from Overflakee island as I re-formed the Wing and set course for home with the golden early morning sun beginning to burn off the mists below. Approx 500 miles, 1 hr 30 mins. Drop tanks retained. No losses.

Tempest bomber escort

Later the same day (11 September) a Form D arrived for a major operation. The Wing was to escort 340 Lancasters and Halifaxes attacking oil storage at Gelsenkirchen in the Ruhr.

This would be at the limit of our range with long-range drop tanks, and if we got into combat over the target or subsequently, some Tempests were not going to get home to Newchurch!

With thirty-six aircraft of all three squadrons taxying out to line up, the dust and dried grass of this long, hot summer was whirled high into a grey pall over Newchurch, and this was increased as pair after pair of Tempests roared off down the bumpy strip.

Although routine after five months of varied and successful operations, the take-off, the first turn on to heading for the enemy coast, the sliding into their positions of the sections and squadrons and the steady climb to operating height, in this case 18,000 ft with the Tempests spread out on either side, were a never failing source of satisfaction.

These thirty-six fighter pilots were highly confident and motivated after their summer at Newchurch, and our Tempests were undoubtedly the best of all fighters for the medium and low altitude war over-the-ground fighting for Europe and beyond into Germany itself. It was a good feeling and the enemy had better watch out!

In fine clear weather the French and Belgian coastline stretched out ahead to the just visible Dutch islands beyond Antwerp. Our course lay across Holland to the Rhine south of Wesel where we would rendezvous with the bomber stream heading into Germany.

In twenty minutes we were in enemy skies over Belgium and keeping a sharp look-out, although radar control reported 'No trade' before we flew beyond VHF range at about 150 nms.

The serenity of the skies viewed to the horizon in all directions through the 360° cockpit vision of our Tempests with the purposeful shapes of the formation all in steady station on either side and behind in the smooth air at our cruising height of 18,000 ft, the silent radio and the now almost-forgotten steady rumble of the big 2000 hp engine almost over my feet, were as always difficult to relate to the sombre purpose of our job.

Frequent automatic glances at the engine, hydraulic and fuel gauges confirmed normality, and continuous checking of visual landmarks against the track and progress times marked on the map confirmed our course. It was my responsibility to lead all these men to an exact rendezvous in time and space 300 miles distant from our take-off point, and furthermore to be able to hand over with precision and accuracy to the deputy leader in the event of my engine failing or any similar occurrence. It was also my job to get them all back safely.

It was an awesome responsibility if you thought about it, but I didn't any more and concentrated on the job in hand. Navigation was solely by watch and map, so it helped to be able to see the ground and on this fine clear day weather was no problem.

The Dutch islands were no longer in sight to port but Eindhoven appeared on time to the left of track and there ahead was the Rhine — our first Wing operation deep into Germany!

Still no sign of EA or flak in the peaceful sky — it seemed unreal.

A check of the chronometer against my fuel gauges confirmed that we were close to the drop point for our LR tanks, as the tail-enders would have used more fuel than those in front.

'Harlequin leader prepare to drop tanks — 5, 4, 3, 2, 1 Go!' On my warning they would all position themselves clear from any possible collision with tanks falling from those ahead.

My tanks went with their normal slight thump, and then without moving the throttle the ASI increased slowly by about 10 mph. Good, we were now in full fighting order for any 190s or 109s.

The wide Rhine was passing under the nose now and the flight plan said that we had eight minutes to go to the rendezvous. The sky was still crystal clear ahead and I began to worry — could I have boobed — what if the bombers did not show up?

But then, with the suddenness that is always a surprise, the empty visibility ahead changed to an indistinct but dark line of cloud across our heading and at our altitude. But why did it look dark?

Then gradually taking shape at probably twenty miles ahead, one, two, six, then dozens of black bombers in a stream from left to right as far as the eye could see, and all round the leaders a dense black cloud of smoke with intermittent flashes and, as we rapidly closed the distance, individual mushrooming bursts of heavy flak.

The bomber force was making its run into the Gelsenkirchen target exactly on time and had already been ranged by the formidable 88-mm flak defences of the Ruhr. The bombers flew on relentlessly into this enormous barrage, and as I turned the Wing slowly to starboard to take up position about 1 mile south of the Lancasters and 500 ft above their level to give ourselves tactical advantage against any *Luftwaffe* attack, it seemed that the barrage was creeping towards us and individual shell bursts were getting uncomfortably close.

But our purpose was to support the courageous bomber crews and I felt that they would not appreciate seeing their fighter escort moving away out of flak range, so I held course parallel to them and now in amongst the shell bursts, conscious of the strong possibility of hits and of the certain criticisms of my leadership which would emerge in debriefing! What had happened to my repeated briefings that they should stay away from the flak whenever possible!

Then it happened. An enormous flash and a mushrooming cloud of black smoke showed amongst the nearest Lancasters on our port side as one of them took a direct hit. In an instant a ball of flame rolled downwards from the formation and small black objects streaming smoke fell away until lost to sight.

The bombers flew on unflinching through the storm of shell-fire, and then another massive flash as a Halifax's bomb-load exploded leaving nothing but smoke and a fireball with a hail of falling debris.

We had joined them over Wesel and now, ahead of us, a carpet of flashing explosions occurred on the ground in the Gelsenkirchen area as the leaders marked the target, and then followed a continuous series of eruptions as bomber after bomber unloaded on the markers.

The bombing looked most impressive, but with fuel down to our minimum for the return to base and our planned fifteen minutes with the bombers over the target now exceeded as far as I dared, I called, 'Turning starboard on to 230° in 1 min', to give the three squadrons time to anticipate and settle down.

We had seen no enemy fighters but I had hoped to give those brave souls of Bomber Command some comfort, and then as I began to turn away from the flak-ringed bombers with the target area below them billowing with smoke clouds towering up thousands of feet, another four-engined bomber broke downwards and away from the main force, streaming a plume of orange fire and black

85

smoke. It could not last long, and suddenly it seemed to stop dead and disintegrate in thousands of fragments fluttering down from the sky.

In those three incidents over twenty valiant aircrew must have died, and those were only a small proportion of the Bomber Command losses that day.

I settled the Wing on its new heading homeward-bound with only marginal fuel left to get us there. The black clouds of battle were still in sight behind and I knew that the Tempest pilots were feeling as I was the frustration of being so close to the 'bomber boys' and having no opportunity to help them.

I also learnt afterwards of other emotions in the Wing when someone said at debriefing, 'That bloody awful flak was the worst I've ever seen — when the Wingco called, "Turn on to reciprocal in one minute" he found he wasn't leading the Wing any more — he was the one at the back!'

It was not true of course, but I was glad to hear that they had all felt as I did!

Log book entry: Wing bomber escort to Gelsenkirchen. 600 miles, 2 hrs 10 mins. No claims/no losses. Tanks dropped.

Tempests against the V2s

The next major Wing operation was on the 13 September.

This was another pre-dawn take-off with twenty-four aircraft of 486 and 3 Squadrons for a set-piece attack on a confirmed V2 launching site in Holland north of The Hague.

The Form D gave the map co-ordinates of the target and orders that if a recognizable target was not identifiable, then the co-ordinates pin-point was to be strafed.

It seemed that the pin-point was in a wood enclosed

on two sides by roads converging to a junction, and thus easy to identify. Strong flak defences were likely.

The taxying, line-up and pairs stream-take-off in the dark were all routine by now, but I was glad of good visibility under half-cloud cover, and similar conditions forecast for the target area.

In fact the cloud dispersed below as we passed along the now familiar route at 10,000 ft with Ostend, Antwerp and the Dutch islands all clearly seen in the spreading sunrise.

Then the Hook of Holland and The Hague to port and the eastern shore of the Zuider Zee to starboard, all the time searching the sky for 109s and 190s but none appeared.

I now eased the formation down towards 5000 ft to gain a closer view of the target area as we approached at about 400 mph (true). There had been no radar warning of enemy activity before we lost VHF contact after 150 miles, and the skies ahead looked empty. The fields, dykes and lakes of Holland were deceptively peaceful in the now warm early morning sunshine.

The last twenty miles run-in required very accurate map reading if we were to find the indistinct target, but exactly on time there was a lake and an adjacent railway line that I had marked as lead-in features at five miles to go — and there ahead on the port side was my V-shaped wood with its converging roads.

Calling 'Going left' I turned the formation over the top through 180° and looked hard for signs of activity in the wood which seemed fairly dense and lacking in buildings of any kind; then I saw indistinct tracks of vehicles entering the wood from a field on one side, and what seemed to be the shadowy path of a number of tracks or roadways in the wood itself.

We had been advised that the V2 and launchers would

be heavily camouflaged, so I decided that I had identified the correct target area and that we would go in and strafe it.

I called, 'Harlequin Leader, the target area is in the centre of the wood bounded by those two roads. I am going to mark the aiming point — all aircraft take that as target, but deal with any flak you see. Echelon starboard Go, all aircraft break left after firing and rejoin on the climb. Don't fire until your next ahead is clear.'

As this had to be a precision job without an obvious target I throttled back slightly to give 350–400 mph in the 30° dive to attack — a modest speed for optimum gun-aiming in a long continuous burst.

With the wood looming large in my windscreen I steadied the aiming spot at a point of convergence of two apparent tracks and, opening fire at about 700 yds, I maintained the burst right down to the level of the tree-tops and into the cloud of smoke and debris thrown up by my shells.

Pulling out very close to the tree-tops I saw a flash and felt a thud and wondered momentarily if I had taken a hit. Then sparks of machine-gun tracer fire flew past.

Now banking left and into a climbing turn I looked back at the stream of Tempests diving and firing at what was now a massive conflagration in the wood. Then suddenly another explosion of fire and a rising ball of shock-wave in the early morning humidity.

That seemed conclusive and as there was a lot of light flak and we were all low in ammunition after long bursts, I decided that that was enough and rocked my wings for the re-join. There was some confused R/T chatter and a 3 Squadron call-sign said, 'That was the CO [S/Ldr K. A. Wigglesworth DFC] — he went straight into the target.'

I asked if he was sure and he said, 'I was his No. 2, and Christ, he went straight in just in front of me.'

There was nothing anyone could do, and it was with a heavy heart that I re-grouped the formation and set course in the now brilliant morning back across the Dutch islands to the Channel coast and home. We would not see Wiggy again.

The remainder landed safely at Newchurch with some minor hits to two Tempests, and Intelligence later confirmed that 'agents' had reported destruction of a V2 site by our attack at that time and place.

Log book entry: Wing attack on V2 site N of The Hague, left on fire. 1 hr 45 mins. 500+ miles. Drop tanks retained. Lost No. 3 squadron CO.

Tempests to 2nd TAF

On 16 September I received notification of an imminent movement of the Wing — we were going to join 2nd TAF at an advanced forward base in Holland!

The ground forces had only just advanced from Antwerp through Eindhoven to the Reichwald forest. The abortive attack at Arnhem was still in progress and would leave the army consolidating a front from Nijmegen to Cleve. We were to move eventually to Volkel only eleven miles from the most advanced army positions, but first to prepare the Wing, update all servicing and bring aircraft and pilot complements up to establishment. My old friend Digby (Digger) Cotes-Preedy was about to replace Bobby Hall as CO of 56 Squadron, and Harvey Sweetman (NZ) had taken over 3 Squadron.

The work was to be carried out at Matlaske in Norfolk, and we were preparing to move there when on 20 September I received an immediate movement order to Manston to stand by for support operations over Arnhem.

I took the opportunity to marshal a maximum effort

formation, and the Wing took off from Newchurch for the last time mustering sixty aircraft of all three squadrons.

I briefed them to form up after normal stream take-off in squadrons each with three sections of four aircraft in line astern, and then to close in to Wing formation of five squadrons line-astern.

The pilots were all well drilled and experienced by now and made an excellent job of it, such that we arrived over Manston in splendid mass formation which clearly impressed the station.

Our servicing Wing was ready to receive us (the result of more efficient organization by 'Digger' Aitken and his headquarters staff), and I was able to declare the first squadron ready for operations within one hour of landing.

But severe weather now intervened and for the whole of the next day we were weathered-in by fog and unable to take part in that tragic operation at Arnhem.

Finally on 27 September I flew RP-B in very marginal weather to Matlaske, and later the same day the three squadrons arrived independently from Manston.

There was no flying for the next five days while the engineers had a field day, except that on 27 September I flew RP-B, with Johnny Iremonger of 486, to Brussels Grimbergen to check out our interim new base in Belgium.

It was a strange experience to cross the North Sea and over the coast of Belgium with the knowledge that this was no longer enemy territory, although we had been well briefed to steer clear of Dunkirk which was still in German hands. The *Luftwaffe* were reported to have withdrawn from all their French and Belgian bases during the past week, to avoid being overrun by the on-rushing Allied armies and to strengthen the homeland defences of the Reich. Nevertheless, it still seemed prudent to keep one's eyes skinned!

After checking the suitability of the just-long-enough all-grass airfield of Grimbergen on the north-west outskirts of Brussels and the available accommodation — our mess was to be a château which had housed *Luftwaffe* fighter pilots until five days previously — it was time to go and we flew back over the North Sea to Matlaske at our Tempest's exhilarating maximum cruise speed of 345 mph IAS at 5000 ft, faster that is than the cruise speeds of the P47s, P51s and all the Spitfires of that period.

Back home all was maximum activity — the Wing Movement was signalled for 0800 hrs the next day! There was just time for the pilots to have a celebratory 'wing-ding' during which Bobby Hall, who was celebrating his posting from 56, on behalf of the Wing presented me with a finely engraved silver tankard recording our Tempest summer of 150 Wing — a heartwarming moment only slightly deflated when I found that it had been half filled with Cointreau and I was expected to down it in one go!

The morning of 28 September was grey and wet with a cold wind off the North Sea as I briefed the Wing. Fifty-four Tempests were available, with others still on major servicing for engine changes or repair work; but I intended that Brussels should see our arrival in style.

The plan was four squadrons of twelve aircraft with a V of three pairs at the rear, and if any of the pilots had hang-overs like mine we were going to need that long straight leg across the North Sea to get together properly — and full oxygen would not do us any harm either!

At 0930 hrs I led out the long gaggle in RP–B on to the undulating and wet grass of Matlaske, and after take-off during which my drop tanks self-jettisoned as we crossed the boundary hedge — I never found out why — I set up a wide circuit at 2000 ft and watched the squadrons forming up and cutting across inside the turn to close into 'squadrons line-astern'.

Setting course over the Norfolk coast for Belgium I called, 'Open out, aircraft search formation-Go' and then climbed the formation towards the cloud base which was above 4000 ft. Three and a half thousand would be fine for the cruise, but I hoped that visibility and cloud base would stay good for our arrival over the Belgian capital.

All went well and after forty minutes and with five minutes to go to the outskirts of Brussels I saw the country-side ahead change character as houses and factories appeared through my left windscreen panel, and then the larger buildings and spires of the city itself.

Calling 'Harlequin Leader [we were still No. 150 Wing at this point and did not take on the call-sign of No. 122 Wing until operating from B6 Airfield Grimbergen] all air-craft close up and squadrons tight line-astern. Turning port for a straight run across base at 1000 ft for the break. Go.'

They knew what to do, and I entered this manoeuvre with fifty-four aircraft confident that they would do it well. But I still had to lead accurately and I had not yet picked out Grimbergen which I was looking for as a narrow patch of green contrasting with the grey and black buildings of the northern suburbs of Brussels on either side of the main road to Ghent.

But there it was suddenly and we were nicely placed to turn in as planned for a run from the east. Holding the turn rate until Grimbergen airfield slid into my windscreen about five miles ahead, I called, 'Levelling out and descending to 1000 ft at this throttle setting. After fly-past, on my call "breaking left", squadrons to echelon starboard, air-craft echelon starboard for normal stream landing. Give yourselves plenty of room and if anyone's in doubt, go round again! Make this good.'

I looked round both sides behind and could see the Tempests of No. 3 close in under my tail-wheel. Behind and below I could also see the wing tips of the next squadron but the rest were out of my vision range. I was sure they were in position as no one had reported diffi- culty.

Here was the grass airfield spreading out ahead now, and we were heading down the centre of it straight towards the city. I did not have formal over-flying author- ity, but the British army had only just captured the place so what the hell!

Holding course for a few more minutes I wheeled the mass formation left over the city centre and called, 'Breaking left. Echelon starboard for landing, Go', and looking over my right shoulder watched as the squadrons and then the individual aircraft fanned out to the right. It was impressive to see so many Tempests, but they still had to be got down safely.

I throttled gently and as the speed settled to 120 mph I called, 'U/c Go!' It wouldn't be necessary to call the flaps as all the pilots would know that these would be lowered as each aircraft turned Finals.

Now I was turning gently on to a left offset final approach to give room to the others behind and with my No. 2 close behind on my starboard side I rolled wings level over the boundary, eased back the throttle, floated gently on to a 'wheeler' landing and kept rolling because of the others behind.

At the far end of the strip I turned right to taxy with my No. 2 and could see that the rest of No. 3 Squadron were rolling and bumping down the field or just approach- ing over the hedge, while the sky beyond was dotted with the next two squadrons curving into the approach.

Overhead came the last squadron and the tail-end V of six aircraft as their leaders correctly elected to make another safe circuit before joining the queue downwind.

It all looked most professional, and as the last line- astern of Tempests came down the approach after I

93

had switched off my engine at the dispersal area, more than forty Tempests came spluttering and coughing across the grass of the foreign airfield, and I felt proud of them.

Air Vice-Marshal Harry Broadhurst came to welcome his new Wing that afternoon and had some pungent comments to make about our recent forced retention in the UK for 'Home Guard' duties against the flying-bombs — but I had already sent off Digger Cotes-Preedy's 56 Squadron on armed reconnaissance and before 'Broady' left I was able to show him an Intelligence signal reporting that 56 Squadron were engaged over the Reichwald forest and claiming three FW-190s!

Our stay in Brussels lasted only six days in which we were fully occupied with sorties over the British sector battle area at squadron strength by day, and by sorties in Jeeps and my 'captured' Delahaye coupé into Brussels to sample the night life (rather rough!) and experience the political turmoil that was following the very recent liberation.

On the morning of 24 September I led 486 Squadron to the Nijmegen battle area and we had a quiet patrol at 10,000 ft under some high stratus cloud but with good visibility below it and the smoke and explosions of the battle area in clear view along the Reichwald forest.

After about one hour's patrolling with no activity, radar control gave 'possible bandits east of you at 10 miles, height unknown'.

Then, 'confirmed Bandits, 20 plus ahead of you now on reciprocal and closing'.

This sounded like a controlled intercept and I called, 'Keep your eyes skinned ahead and above.' Radar then said, 'The plots are merging — they are close to you, probably same height.' I acknowledged, and then suddenly across our front from right to left and about 2000 ft above appeared a long straggling formation of fighters which must have just emerged from the bottom of the stratus cloud.

Rounded wing tips and stubby noses identified them as 109s, and as I counted 20–30 and began turning my formation in towards them I called, 'Tally-ho, targets at 12 o'clock high, turning in after them and opening up.'

The enemy outnumbered us and had height advantage, but we had the better aeroplanes so I felt confident in climbing up from our disadvantaged position into attack from behind and below if I could get there, or to take them head-on if they rolled back into a pass at us.

Neither of these things happened. After a full 360° turn climbing from 10 — 14,000 ft, still in their straggling formation the 109s were perhaps 1000 yds nearer but still matching our rate of turn and climbing above us.

They apparently did not want to use their advantage and, realizing that we were gaining on them, they suddenly rolled out wings level streaming black over-boost smoke and climbing more steeply.

Conscious that we were getting low on fuel, I opened up fully to try to get at least a long-range shot at the untidy enemy formation which was now only about 700 yds ahead. Another few minutes and we would catch them — and then one after the other they became blurred and finally disappeared just ahead of us as they climbed into the cloud sheet!

We had no chance at them now and I turned away for home, but with my fuel down to about thirty minutes I called the others and said we were about twenty minutes from Grimbergen (in economic cruise descent from 17,000 ft) and anyone who couldn't make it should head for Antwerp (just recently captured and about twelve minutes from our present position).

Three tail-enders did this safely, and the rest of us

landed at Grimbergen with very little fuel left. The Antwerp section rejoined us later saying that when they got out at Antwerp they found it under heavy (and far too close) V1 attack and also long-range 88-mm fire, and they were quite glad to leave!

Our final movement forward to Volkel (B80 airfield in Holland) took place on 1 October; another day of heavy cloud with a cold north-east wind and rain showers, and because of the proximity of enemy positions to within three miles of the eastern perimeter of the airfield and of the relatively narrow cleared approach to it up the Dutch salient, I sent the squadrons separately and flew in myself solo.

In the last five minutes of this flight I received a noisy direct hit to my starboard tailplane from light flak — I was letting down through 2000 ft over what I thought was 'friendly' territory and only about five miles south of Volkel. But control was not affected, and when I landed and taxied in on the brick runways and taxyways of this big ex-*Luftwaffe* (last week!) base it was to find that W/O Reid of 3 Squadron had also been fatally hit on his approach to land, and that RP-B would need a new tailplane.

This clearly was a very operational base which showed evidence on all sides of having been overrun in a fierce battle. All hangars and buildings were reduced to rubble with here and there signs visible in still-standing walls, '*Rauchen Verboten*'!

The wreckage of many Horsa gliders and C-47 tugs were scattered around the western dispersals with Tempests now parked amongst them, and here and there the small mounds of hastily dug graves.

Roadways on the airfield and just outside on the main road to Uden were littered with the burnt-out wrecks of armoured vehicles already red with rust; and in moments

Ground-attack fighter 1918. The Sopwith Camel was the first fighter to be successfully employed in large-scale 'ground strafing' operations. (Imperial War Museum)

Ground-attack fighter 1941. The second prototype Hawker Typhoon with the much criticised lack of rear vision, before the role change from interceptor fighter which began in 1942. (British Aerospace Archive)

The author's Typhoon 1b, serial R7752, when commanding 609(WR) Squadron. Manston 1942/43. (Zeigler)

The prototype Hawker Tempest V, serial HM595, with Typhoon-style cockpit and tail, tested by the author in 1943. (British Aerospace Archive)

First stage modification of the Tempest fin to improve directional stability.
(British Aerospace Archive)

The first series production Tempest V with the final fin configuration. The author flew over fifty test flights in the clearance programme of this aircraft. Note the excellent all-round view from the new sliding cockpit canopy. (British Aerospace Archive)

Another view of the VN729 on Hawker's Langley test airfield in 1943 with production Hurricane IIs and a Typhoon on engine-runs in the background. (British Aerospace Archive)

'Digger' Cotes-Preedy in a Tempest V series 2 with 'short' cannon, from Langley in 1945. Cotes-Preedy had commanded No. 56 Squadron with Tempests at Volkel before being 'rested' at Hawkers. (British Aerospace Archive)

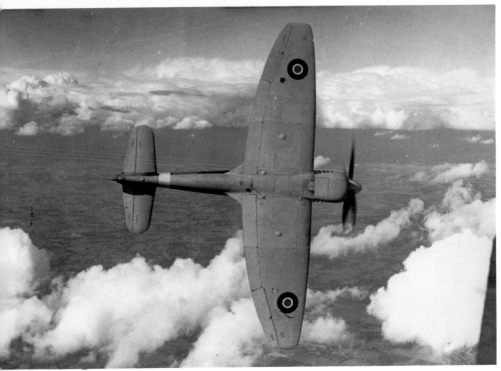

A classic Cyril Peckham picture capturing the new wing shape of the Tempest which could quite easily be mistaken for a Spitfire XIV, though not for a 190 or 109, even though it often was by trigger-happy Allied fighters! (British Aerospace Archive)

The second production Tempest V at Langley in late 1943 before delivery by the author to Boscombe Down for service trials. (British Aerospace Archive)

A factory-fresh Tempest V delivered in early 1944 to the first squadron to receive them, No. 486(NZ) and seen here at Castle Camps in March 1944. The first Air Ministry photo-call on the new Tempests. (Imperial War Museum)

The author's Tempest V in March 1944 with Wing-leader's initials and showing clearly the gunsight directly reflected in the windscreen – the 'Beamont' modification. (Imperial War Museum)

A 486 Squadron Tempest in a low flypast at Castle Camps, March 1944.
(Imperial War Museum)

A Tempest of 3 Squadron at Newchurch in summer 1944 with a section returning from V1 ('Diver') patrol overhead. Note protective cover to prevent scratching of the large clear-view canopy. (Imperial War Museum)

Wing Commander Roland Beamont, OC 150 and 122 Wings, with Squadron Leader Digby Cotes-Preedy, OC 56 Squadron (at Volkel). (Imperial War Museum)

Squadron Leader Alan Dredge, OC 3 Squadron (at Newchurch).
(Imperial War Museum)

Squadron Leader Johnny Iremonger, OC 486(NZ) Squadron. The first Tempest squadron commander (in front of the author's Tempest 'RB').
(Imperial War Museum)

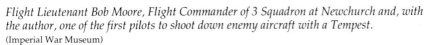

Flight Lieutenant Bob Moore, Flight Commander of 3 Squadron at Newchurch and, with the author, one of the first pilots to shoot down enemy aircraft with a Tempest.
(Imperial War Museum)

'Invasion Stripes'! The author's 'RB'/JN751 repainted for the 'D-Day' invasion with black and white stripes round the rear fuselage and also on the wings. This aircraft, which was also identified by a yellow spinner, scored the first Tempest victory against enemy aircraft, a Bf-109G on 'D-Day plus 2' near the beachhead. (Author)

Bob Cole of No. 3 Squadron surveys rudder burnt by an exploding V1. (Imperial War Museum)

The FW-190 was a formidable fighter but was outclassed by the Tempest V.
(Imperial War Museum)

The first captured FW-190 being flown by Wing Commander 'Willy' Wilson at Farnborough in 1943. This was the first 190 tested by the author, RAF serial MR499.
(Imperial War Museum)

A captured Messerschmitt Bf-109G. (Imperial War Museum)

The Ju-88 G1 night-fighter flown by the author at Tangmere. (Imperial War Museum)

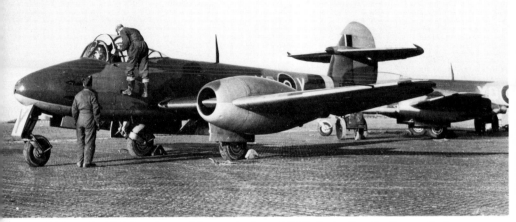

A Meteor I of 616 Squadron at Manston in August 1944. Faster than the Tempest but ineffective against the V1s, shooting down only 13 in the period in which the Tempests shot down over 700. (Imperial War Museum)

Griffon Spitfire 14. The 12 and 14 were the fastest Spitfires against the V1s, but were slower than the Tempest. (Imperial War Museum)

Mustang I with Allison engine. (Imperial War Museum)

Mustang II with Merlin engine. (Imperial War Museum)

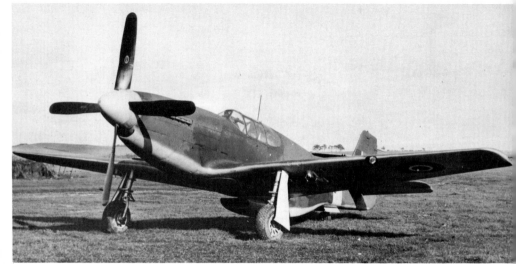

Mustang III with Merlin engine and improved cockpit vision. (Imperial War Museum)

A North American P51D, the ultimate development of the Mustang for the USAAF in WW2. The author with the owner, airline Captain Connie Bowlin, at Maxwell AFB, Alabama, in 1991. (Author)

The prototype Hawker Tempest 2, test-flown by the author at Langley in 1943, with original 'Typhoon' tail before modification to 'Tempest' production standard.
(British Aerospace Archive)

The ultimate RAF multi-role fighter in the final years of WW2. A Tempest V series 1.
(Imperial War Museum)

of quiet when the Sabre engines of Volkel's Tempest and Typhoon Wings (over 100 aircraft) were momentarily not running, the almost continuous sound of gunfire was present.

The ATC complex was tented in the centre of the airfield in the triangle between the runways and, like every other centre of activity, they had slit trenches handy for diving into when under direct attack.

I found that Pat (Jamie) Jameson, the New Zealand Battle of Britain pilot group captain commanding the base, had already located an Intelligence caravan near the Tempest dispersal area for use as Base Intelligence and HQs W/Cdr Flying 122 Wing.

Since our arrival the three squadrons had been reinforced with Nos. 80 and 274 Squadrons, making this Tempest force a valuable new arrival in the British sector. The C-in-C, Harry Broadhurst, had made clear his high expectations of the Tempests and we were determined not to disappoint him.

There was less than adequate time to ensure that we were all settled in properly before our operations from this most advanced RAF main base began, and after a brief discussion with Jamie I had to leave the squadron commanders to sort out their dispersal and billeting arrangements themselves.

Early next day, 2 October, I led 56 Squadron on the first sortie — an air superiority patrol of the Nijmegen-Rhine front at 15,000 ft and from this height, again with high cloud above, we could see the smoke of ground battle and frequent glimpses of the Rhine between the broken clouds below at 2–3000 ft.

We were now under full and effective radar control, mobile radars having been set up immediately following the army's recent advance; but all was quiet for the first forty-five minutes. Then there was a report of jet activity by Me-262s for a while which came to nothing.

Eventually I turned the formation on to a southerly heading to take us back over base at the end of our one-hour patrol, when radar came up with '10–20 probable Bandits east of you, 10 miles, no height.'

Then, 'Trade closing you at 1 o'clock, same height 5 miles.'

Scanning the misty air ahead between the cloud layers I held my heading to hear the next radar call, and then there, ahead and above diving out of the high cloud directly at us, came a series of black dots which rapidly developed at the closing speed of 6–700 mph, into thin wings and round noses — 190s!

As I called, 'Tally-ho, 190s straight ahead port side, breaking left after them', the leaders streamed white smoke as they opened fire apparently at the left of our formation.

They missed and were already streaming past our port side when the leader rolled sharply right into a near verti-cal dive, followed one by one by all his gang. He was pre-senting the Tempests with a perfect target as we had all the advantage of speed in our dive capability! I was already rolling left and pulling down towards them and, with gun-sight switched on and range bar already set for a 30 ft span at 200 yds, I called, 'Down after them — balls out!'

I had selected the nearest 190 in the weaving gaggle ahead, and there was another just off my right wing tip and falling behind fast, apparently hell bent after the others and not bothered about me. At least I just hoped my No. 2 would deal with him if he tried to get in a shot at me.

In this near vertical dive we were already down through 7000 ft and I was catching them fast when I fired a short burst at my target from about 300 yds. Hits and smoke from his wing roots at once and the 190 nosed over to beyond the vertical. At well over 500 mph indicated I rolled easily clearing to the right, and pulled up hard, as the fields and trees now seen through the scattered cloud rushing up from below looked altogether too close at this dive angle and speed — and there below and to port was a flash and eruption of smoke and the white globe of shock wave as the 190 went straight in near Cleve. My No. 2 confirmed this and said, 'We were over 510 when you fired at him!'

The others had not been able to get into firing range in that short, fast dive before the rest of the enemy reached the cover of the lower cloud and we lost them; and then as I called the join-up and began a climbing turn through 7000 ft in the direction of base, a cloud of light flak came up from front-line positions in the Reichwald Forest.

On the way back, with some scanty information from radar warning of 'possible trade', two of 56 Squadron on patrol saw a couple of Me-262s briefly before they ducked into cloud. The Wing would see more of these in the near future.

But the Tempests had opened their score at Volkel* and we had seen a classic example of under-estimation and bad tactics by the enemy — there was no way that a 190 could roll and dive away from combat with a Tempest!

Days followed of low cloud and heavy rain which reduced activity at Volkel, although I was able to lead 486 on an uneventful sweep of the Arnhem area on 6 October.

The next major event occurred on 12 October, a date which proved memorable for me on a number of counts. On the previous evening, Philip Lucas, Hawkers' Chief Test Pilot, had visited us (in a Spitfire which we thought highly amusing!) and over dinner in our ex-girl-school mess that evening with Jamie Jameson and Typhoon Wing

* See Appendix 10.

leader Charles Green, Lucas had mentioned that as my third tour of operations was about to be declared 'expired' (the first that I had heard of it) P Staff (Fighter Command postings branch) were going to post me back to Langley on the Special Duties List as No. 2 experimental test pilot to Bill Humble, and that after the war ended, in the near future I could, if I wished, join Hawkers' testing team as a civilian test pilot.

It all sounded fine to me, but I told Philip I wanted to do a few more sorties from Volkel as the Tempest was really getting its teeth in and I didn't want to miss all of it!

The next morning, another cold grey day of frequent rain showers, we had Form Ds for what were now seen as our regular air superiority patrols at squadron strength, and an additional order for an armed reconnaissance to Münster, primary target Me-262 jet fighter-bombers operating out of Rheine airfield, and secondary 'targets of opportunity'.

This would be mostly at low level and was a fairly deep penetration into Germany, and I felt that I had better lead this one.

So I called their CO Harvey Sweetman from my 'ops' caravan and said that I would lead 3 Squadron and be over for briefing in a few minutes.

Then the Intelligence Officer came in with a signal warning that low-level attacks by Me-262s with anti-personnel cluster bombs had been made at Grave nearby and could be expected at Volkel at any time. The need for slit trenches for all personnel was emphasized. This news provided increased motivation for our trip to Rheine — we would get after those 262s!

At 3 Squadron's crew room in the side offices of a partly destroyed hangar, I gave a quick run-over of our well-tried procedures in relation to this sortie and said that we would circuit Rheine airfield at cloud-base for as long as

100

fuel permitted, hoping to be able to 'jump' 262s either taking off or returning to land. If we had to fly over the airfield flak would be heavy and one or two sections would peel off to 'suppress' the flak. 'Finally,' I said 'if I go for an alternative ground target it will be our usual one-pass-only and then out on the deck to reform after five miles.' In retrospect I wish I had listened to my own briefing!

Then out over the mud and debris-strewn taxyway in a cold grey drizzle — it was not an attractive start to what might become a 'hairy' sortie.

But then the normal routine, brief-words with the ground crew — yes we were going to let Germany have a taste of No. 3 today! Then settle into the cockpit, stow the maps, check the 'Gen' card on my glove for the first course and 'safety course' for home. Engine instruments, fuel, oxygen, hydraulics, brakes, gunsight, VHF — start-up.

I waved my hand overhead and pressed the starter, and the great Sabre engine coughed into acrid life. All was normal and I waved away the cocks and taxied slowly forward looking round to see the others moving out down the line.

The take-off was to be easterly into a fresh wind, and by the time we had weaved round debris and shell-holed patches on the perimeter road and begun to line-up, some eight minutes had elapsed.

When just about to open up I noticed a chain of Bofors shell bursts on the south side of the airfield leading towards us, and there well ahead of them a sleek fast shape running in low across our heading and about one mile away.

It was a 262 jet and as I watched objects detached from its belly and a string of explosions ran across the centre of the airfield, it seemed in the area of the ATC tented control unit.

We felt the shock waves but were in no danger,

although I thought instinctively that he might have a wing man running in directly over us! But this was not so and the 262 lifted into a smooth and still very fast climbing turn and disappeared into the cloud.

I was about to go, but the ATC broke silence and said, 'Runway 08 u/s — use runway 190.' This meant taxying right back to beyond where we had started and we were going to be short of some valuable fuel. But I acknowledged and said, 'Any casualties?' and ATC said, 'Some.'

So off we went in single file round the perimeter again and by the time we were lined up again we had been running engines for twenty wasted minutes. But we could still have a go.

Giving the take-off hand signal I closed my canopy and opening up smoothly to minimise any downwind take-off difficulties, I turned steeply onto our first heading while retracting the u/c, knowing that this experienced mob behind would easily follow and would soon be in search formation.

We crossed the Rhine SW of Wesel with cloud base at about 4000 ft which was quite suitable, and I began to search the ground ahead and on either side of our course. This we knew was an area of maximum troop concentrations and there could be military targets anywhere.

But even so I was surprised when, still only thirty miles from our base, I saw the unmistakable smoke and steam plume of a train. This was broad daylight and we were supposed to have virtual air dominance of this sector, so what was a train doing there?

It turned out to be an important target and changed the priorities, such that when I led the squadron into a third attack on an already devastated target I only then remembered my 'one pass only' briefing!

Pulling up and rocking my wings for the rejoin, my No. 2 came sliding in on my right and called, 'Corncob leader, you are streaming smoke!' I looked at the radiator temperature gauge —it was already off the clock!

Time then stood still as many things happened at once — a call to the deputy leader to take the boys home, and to Volkel (still in R/T range) that I was force-landing. They acknowledged saying, 'Good luck.'

Then concentration on how and where to put this stricken Tempest down — previous belly-landing experiences on Typhoons and Tempests came in handy at this point.

Moments of hectic use of the controls in the last seconds of gliding and side-slipping between tall pine trees into the only (and impossibly small) clearing visible for miles in the forest; and then belly-sliding surprisingly smoothly but much too quickly towards the next belt of towering trees, only to slow up suddenly and undramatically to a stop as yards of post and wire fencing hooked round wings and tailplane as a very effective arrester gear!

A radio call to the others to confirm that I was OK (received by them), and then out on the wing to lean back into the cockpit to set off the incendiary device and set fire to this valuable new fighter which the enemy would have been delighted to receive intact.

It went up with a satisfying roar, and even while all this was going on I kept thinking, 'I've really blown this and who is going to look after things at home?' (I had only just learned of serious family illness).

However the next immediate priority was to evade capture in the hope of a possible air rescue operation that night, but these plans were soon ended by a voice shouting, '*Hande Hoch*' and finding myself looking into the barrel of a Schmeisser machine-pistol held by an eager *Obergefreiter* who seemed over-anxious to use it.

I had accepted with regret that I would have to leave the Tempest Wing, but now I had left it in quite the wrong direction and it was only after the war that I was able to read in a 2nd TAF Intelligence Summary that at the end of hostilities the squadrons of 122 Wing had achieved the highest score against enemy aircraft, equal with a Spitfire Wing, and that at the same time they were recorded as the highest scoring Wing of all against rail transport targets in the period from D-Day to VE Day.

122 Tempest Wing concluded its private war by flying in to Copenhagen in May 1945, and accepting the surrender of the German forces at Castrup airfield! Limited in numbers to one Wing in 1944 and only two Wings (Nos. 122 and 135) by 1945 totalling eight* squadrons, the Tempest V had proved to be the most effective multi-role fighter in the RAF at medium and low altitude, and with arguably the best combination of air-combat and ground-attack capabilities of any allied or enemy fighter in 1944–45.

In the thick of the hardest fighting in the last six months of the war, the Tempest's successes were not achieved without heavy losses of aircraft and pilots, and it is to those largely unsung heroes, many of them my Newchurch friends, that this book is dedicated.

* Nos. 3, 486, 56, 80, 274, 33 and 222 in 2nd TAF, and 501 in UK.

CHAPTER 7

EPILOGUE — TANGMERE
SUMMER 1945

Affter the cease-fire in Europe in May 1945 the Central Fighter Establishment at Tangmere, Sussex was a place of contrasts in July. The main tarmac area in front of the hangars that had survived the dive-bombing in 1940, and the dispersal areas on the east, south and west sides of the big airfield, were congested with fighters of all types including the new Meteor jets and examples of captured enemy aircraft.

But the testing, evaluation and training programmes were slowing down after the end of hostilities, and some were already in abeyance. Everyone it seemed was awaiting new directives, and the majority of personnel were naturally more interested in their demobilization dates than anything else. So that the maintenance of Tangmere's traditional high morale was not easy in the circumstances, however the Commandant, Air Commodore Dick ('Batchy') Atcherley, was not about to let despondency take over!

In early June I had returned from Stalag 3A at Luckenwald together with eight other ex-POWs in a Bomber Command Lancaster, one of hundreds operating out of Brussels Le Culot. It was a hairy flight with a young pilot on his first sortie with his squadron who thought it best to stay under the weather until it clamped on the hills behind Calais which he very nearly hit! Later, after penetrating an overworked and rather unwelcoming POW reception centre at Cosford, I set about establishing a new job before P Staff got a chance to post me on a training course.

A call to 'Batchy' at Tangmere elicited the response, 'What do you want to do, Old Boy?' I said, 'How about some flying?' and he said, 'Got just the job for you. Come and see me tomorrow.'

The Commandant's headquarters was in a grey stone house outside the main base area, tree-surrounded and approached by a weedy gravel drive. The one-time gardens had become overgrown thickets during the years of wartime priorities, but it was pleasantly rural and secluded.

Batchy explained that despite the post-war run-down which was inevitable, he did not intend to miss a unique opportunity to tap and record the mass of experience that was now available before it became dispersed with postings and demobilization.

So he had set up a section within CFE staffed with ex-Wing-leaders or other unit commanders with special areas of experience, and had called it 'The Tactics Branch'.

This outfit, which already contained such stalwarts as Bob Stanford Tuck, Bobby Oxpring, Frank Carey, Robin Johnston, Colin Gray and Pete Brothers was commanded by Douglas Bader and had as its terms of reference 'to evaluate the characteristics of fighters relevant to specialist roles, and to review and revise tactics for all fighter operations'. Batchy didn't need to ask the question, 'Want to join us?'

I soon found that my hilarious colleagues were preoccupied with the review of tactics as a first priority, and we were also all to take part in the RAF interrogation of some of the recently-captured German 'Experten' including Adolf Galland and Hans Ülrich Rudel, but the field was open to me to begin the type-evaluations; so June and July became busy and interesting months.

In the next six weeks I flew three German types FW-190, Bf-109G6, Ju-88GI (night fighter) and, for comparison, Meteor III, Spitfire IX, XVI and XIV, Mustang IV (P51D) and Tempest V and II.

The briefings for some of these 'conversions' could be described as rudimentary, consisting mainly of two pages of 'Pilot's Notes' and self-authorization in the relevant unit authorization book. Personal briefings by a type-experienced pilot seldom happened — and never in the case of German aircraft!

However I had flown all the marks of Spitfire before and also the Meteor, FW-190 and both Tempests, so only the 109, Mustang IV (I had flown a Mk I) and the Ju-88 were completely new to me.

After seven months incarceration as a guest of the Third Reich I needed to get back into practice, and I set about this by using aircraft for necessary travel wherever possible.

For example on 4–5 June I took a Spitfire IX to Condover to visit an old school-friend back from a nasty war in Burma. Then a Tempest 2 serial MW745 to Cosford on 12 June for post-POW medical board. ('The officer shall not travel by air' said the movement order.)

At Cosford a young '1st tour' medical officer decided that my category was A2HBH (instead of A1). I thanked him and said, 'What does that mean?' and he said, 'Unfit to fly.' This, he said, was an eyesight problem due to 'reduced muscle-balance' following captivity and a period of starvation diet. 'How would I recognize this?' I said. 'If you flew you'd find it difficult to land,' he said. 'I didn't notice that here this morning,' I said.

He looked rather pained at this and referred me to the wing-commander president of the board who was

107

more interested and also said that I really shouldn't fly. So I said, 'Alright,' went out and flew my Tempest back to Tangmere; and I still wasn't experiencing any vision problems.

There followed some rather stern messages which culminated in a civilised interview with the Chief RAF Medical Officer at Adastral House in which he said, 'Go ahead and fly' but let him know if I had any vision problems at all. I thanked him but didn't think it prudent to tell him that I had flown four different types of fighter during that week, one of them at night!

To be fair the medical services were having to screen thousands of returning aircrew in a short period, and so were tending to deal with cases strictly 'by the book'.

Neither I nor my colleagues were in patient or over-cautious moods at this period and we were inclined to 'buck the system' if it didn't appear to be working efficiently, and probably because of this it was not long before some of us were sent on the OATS (Officers Advanced Training School) course at Cranwell to sort out our post-war discipline! But in the meantime there was all this interesting flying.

After eight sorties on Spitfires IX and XIV and Tempests V and 2, I was ready for the evaluation programme which I had been free to define and set up for myself! So on 26 June I began the first with FW-190 serial EA44 of the Enemy Aircraft Flight.

The first 190 to be captured intact had landed, in error the pilot Amin Faber had said, at RAF Pembry in 1943; and on 13 September that year I had flown it and reported on it (RAF serial PN999, at Farnborough):

> . . . there was an immediate impression of power and strength with simplicity of line and proportion.

108

The short squat fuselage and high main under-carriage suggested that ground stability might be a problem, which it certainly was later.

To the fighter pilot a major point of interest was the clear rear-vision canopy which was a superb one-piece moulded transparency and gave practical rear vision down to below the tailplane on both sides (a unique facility for the period, until the arrival into service of the Typhoon and Tempest clear view canopy in 1943/44. These were followed with redesigned canopies for the P47 and P51 and later marks of Spitfire in 1944, and not before time).

Once settled into the cockpit there was an immediate impression that it exactly fitted the fighter pilot.

This was the first example of a fighter cockpit 'furnished' with the two side consoles and centre main panel arrangement (which survives to this day even with EFIs) with a logical economic layout, and it had the notable advantage of electrical trimming in pitch through stick-switch operation.

All control runs were push-rod operated, and smooth and back-lash free through low coefficient of friction circuits; and even before start-up the 190 gave an impression of unusually high standards of engineering.

The engine started easily and rumbled smoothly with much acrid exhaust smoke while taxying, and there was a noticeable tendency to swing into the ground-loop which needed firm anticipation and, when necessary as it very often was, pulling the stick hard back into tail-wheel castoring lock to stop the swing. This was an essential action during any landing run.

Take-off was straightforward with reaction from

the big propeller easily countered with rudder. The contrast in view from the steep tail-down position to that in the take-off attitude was striking, and suddenly any sensation of restriction of awkwardness was gone in this high-sitting wide-field-of-view cockpit with controls and instruments easily reached or seen, and the 190 leapt off the short N/S runway at Farnborough into a strong southerly wind feeling every inch a fighter aeroplane.

This impression increased throughout the flight; light, responsive and dead-beat lateral control gave a high rate of roll at combat speeds and only heavied-up significantly above about 500 kph. The elevator control was in good harmony with ailerons and light enough and well damped enough to pull high 'g' easily without over-controlling, and the rudder was unobtrusive but satisfactory for countering the directional changes resulting from sharp power variations with the big BMW engine.

The latter itself was smooth and responsive to throttle, and clearly maintained power and a high rate of climb at 30,000 ft where it seemed likely to create problems for even the latest marks of Spitfire.

Rolling into dives the 190 gained speed rapidly while retaining dead-beat directional damping, and the gunsight bead could be placed firmly on a simulated target and then tracked accurately throughout the speed range checked from about 300 to 550 kph IAS.

From low level to 20,000 ft in high rate rolls, tight turns, steep climbing turns and wing-overs it proved to be a formidable fighter aeroplane and attractive to fly with visibility all round which had great operational significance, and it was only in the accelerated stall which produced a sharp wing-drop and in the steep ground attitude and proneness to swing violently on landing that serious criticisms could be made.

When settling into the currently traditional curved approach on to 'finals' for the Farnborough short runway I was very reluctant to bring back this extremely pleasant and potent fighter which I felt would give us many headaches in the months ahead in the hands of experienced pilots.

But I also felt that inexperienced pilots might have trouble with it, and it was comforting to realize that the Typhoon would probably out-turn and out-perform it at heights below 20,000 ft, while the latest Spitfire (Mk ix) could probably just about match it in performance at 30,000 ft though not below.

FW-190 EA44 1 June 1945

On 1 June 1945 in my second sortie in a 190 I planned to confirm these first impressions or discover any new ones in the light of experience in the two intervening years of testing and combat with the Tempest V.

Take-off in EA44 from Tangmere was straightforward with the need to correct swing with rudder, and once again there was this immediate feeling of eager performance and agility with quality engineering. A fine, precise fighter with excellent manoeuvrability, climb performance and tracking (gun-aiming) capability, but somehow a little less impressive than it had been in 1943.

EA44 had been fitted with a mph ASI for direct performance comparison, and it was immediately apparent that from ground level to 20,000 ft the 190 was about 50 mph slower than a Tempest V. From there up to 35,000 ft it maintained performance well and would out-perform a Tempest above 30,000 ft and it would match a Spitfire IX and XIV at that height, but not in turning performance. Above 30,000 ft both Spitfires were faster.

However it had one clear shortfall. At its Vne (dive limit) of 500 mph IAS (approx) the controls were noticeably heavier and rate of roll slowing, whereas the Tempest V was unaffected and with high rate roll remaining at its Vne of 545 mph — the highest dive speed of any conventional fighter of the period.

This was significant as the Spitfires IX and XIV were limited to 450 and 465 mph IAS respectively and only the P51D (and Mustang III) had a higher limit at 485 mph IAS, and of course it had been the standard tactic of the *Luftwaffe* in 1944–45 to make one firing-pass attack and then roll into a vertical dive away.

The 190s could often get away with this from Spitfires, Mustangs and Thunderbolts, but they could not from the Tempests as No. 150 Wing had first proved in 1944, or from Typhoons at fairly low level.

But comparative performance aside this was a taut, potent and altogether likeable fighter aeroplane with the qualities to make it a favourite with fighter pilots with its excellent vision and high manoeuvrability; with a precision feel about the controls, stable gun aiming, and performance and controllability to out-dive most aircraft on the Allied side of 1944 and all German fighters except the not-yet-in-service Messerschmitt and Arado jets.

As I dived EA44 back into the Tangmere circuit enjoying every minute in this fighter pilot's fighter, I recalled writing in 1943 '... it would be no bad thing to be in a 190 squadron at this time, but we'll be able to see it off with the Tempest' —and that had proved to be an accurate forecast.

Meteor Mk III Serial EE241 11 July 1945

I next renewed acquaintance with a Meteor Mk III, serial EE241 (first series with Welland engines) on 11 July.

My first jet experience had been at Manston with Meteor I, VQ-I of 616 Squadron on 26 August 1944. This was at the height of the flying-bomb battle in which my Tempests were heavily involved at nearby Newchurch, and although impressed by the turbine smoothness and the easy-to-land tricyle undercarriage, I had not found the heavy controls, restricted manoeuvrability and poor visibility from the heavily framed windscreen and canopy, together with very restricted endurance, at all suitable for fighter combat at that stage of the war. It had a 70 mph speed advantage at low level over the Tempest, but that and the undercarriage were in my view the only points in its favour. I did not feel that it would do well either against the flying-bombs or in air superiority (Combat Air Patrol) fighting.

In this Meteor at Tangmere I flew a representative sortie climbing to 30,000 ft, diving to 530 mph IAS (below 15,000 ft to avoid compressibility which was not our immediate interest), assessing combat manoeuvres, and finally assessing gun-aiming tracking in simulated ground attacks before the fuel crisis demanded immediate landing after about thirty-five minutes.

In all these I again found the turbine smoothness and power impressive, and it was obviously useful to be able to reach 500 mph IAS in only a shallow dive. But at this speed, as for much of the flight envelope, the controls were so heavy as to be most unsuitable for fighter combat. Gun-aiming was also marred by continuous 'snaking' and by low directional damping in turbulence.

Again it was interesting to fly with jet power which was clearly going to be the path for the future, but it

113

seemed unlikely that the Meteor heavy twin would have sufficient potential for development into a competitive combat fighter. In the CFE assessment at that point in summer 1945 there had been no aspects of fighter operations in the recent conflict which could not be better undertaken by the P51, Tempest and Ta152 generation of piston-engined fighters; but we added the reservation that the Me-262, which we had not tested, could well have some major advantages in the areas of the Meteor's shortfalls.

BF-109G6 RAF serial VD349 12 July 1945

Since first seeing 'Emils' in France in 1940 and having close looks at one in combat over Lyme Bay in August 1940 just before it belly-landed on fire near Abbotsbury, and at another (Gustav) over Rouen in 1944, I had wondered how the *Luftwaffe* could cope with what seemed to be very restricted vision from the cockpit.

'Gustav' VD349 still retained the original windscreen and side-hinged canopy arrangement, and as I settled into the narrow cockpit which fitted tightly at the shoulders and closed and locked the canopy, there was an immediate feeling of claustrophobia — first impressions had been correct! Vision out of this small aeroplane was difficult even for taxying.

The cockpit layout was primitive after the tailored 190, and showed evidence of its production development through many sub-series with an abundance of add-on instruments and brackets.

The DB engine was rough and raucous after the 190's BMW801, and taxying required a weaving path similar to all Spitfires in order to see round the long nose.

A gusting south-westerly wind caused the 109 to rock

114

gently on its narrow undercarriage, and frequent use of the full-back-stick tail-wheel lock was needed to stop incipient swinging. The 109 felt touchy from the start.

Following the briefing notes carefully I increased power progressively during the take-off, easing the stick forwards to raise the tail at about 60 mph and countering swing with the rudder which became effective at quite low speed.

The G6 became airborne at about 70 mph with only slight aft stick and immediately gave the impression of being a hot little ship. The big engine thundered in front, with light and delicate ailerons on the climb at 165 mph. All-round vision was severely restricted by the heavy windscreen and armour-glass frames in front with Revi gunsight in the middle, by the sideways and upwards view through small square transparencies in the metal-framed hood, and the vital rearwards vision was virtually non-existent. All this gave a first impression of rushing along in a tunnel, and it was only when checking ASI and altimeter that the performance was actually seen to be less than impressive.

Up to 25,000 ft (British ASI and altimeter fitted) level performance was at least 50 mph down on the Tempest V, but at 30,000 ft and above the gap was closed and the G6 clearly had superior climb performance above about 15,000 ft. But there its advantages ended.

In turning manoeuvre it was similar to the Tempest up to 20,000 ft but in rate of roll it could only match the Tempest up to about 350 mph IAS. After that the ailerons heavied up rapidly and at anything over 450 mph they were virtually solid! This was no fighter to match the 545 mph IAS manoeuvrability of the Tempest, or even the 485 limit of the Mustang.

As expected with its slim, high fineness-ratio fuselage and adequate fin and rudder area, directional

115

damping was crisp and it had the makings of a good gun-platform.

Combat manoeuvres in the 250–350 mph range were good, but above that the heavy ailerons were soon severely limiting and in hard turning below 200 mph IAS the stall boundary was approached with heavy and disturbing wing rocking caused by asymmetric leading edge slot operation.

As I winged over back down into the Tangmere circuit, I felt that this aeroplane had little to commend it by comparison with its Allied contemporaries, with the exception of its famous fuel injection system which gave it superior negative 'G' capability.

Setting up a standard curved 'Spitfire Approach' seemed quite natural in this long-nosed fighter. The undercarriage and flaps went down without exceptional trim change, and the final turn to wings-level over the threshold in a light cross-wing from port felt tight and secure although the fact that the side-hinged canopy could not be slid back in the fashion of the time was irksome; and then for the complication.

Flaring and throttling back at about 85 mph the crosswind made itself felt and I instinctively decided on a 'wheeler', keeping the tail level until the main wheels touched before beginning to lower the tail wheel.

But the Gustav was not about to settle for this and despite countering with aileron and rudder, the crosswind caused the starboard main wheel to touch first with a squeal, and this resulted in a gentle series of bounces which were eventually ironed out tail-high until the speed decayed and lowered the tail wheel into contact when immediate tail-wheel lock was needed to keep straight.

This aeroplane was unforgiving, so I called the Tower for clearance, took off and tried it again — with similar results! In no way would this aircraft accept either 'wheeler' or three-point landings on a runway with a 10 kts crosswind without protest, and it was clear that grass-field operation permitting take-offs and landings directly into wind would be an operational necessity if landing accidents were to be held to a minimum. This was, of course, the experience of all 109 operators throughout the war years in which the landing accident rate had been seriously high.

I taxied the Gustav back to dispersal with wings rocking delicately on its narrow undercarriage, and weaving it from side-to-side for forward vision amid gusts of exhaust smoke.

Not a good fighter by comparison with the Allies' best, but a capable one in the hands of a good pilot and one which, I supposed, could have found favour with pilots who had not experienced anything better. But I at least would not have enjoyed going to war in one with that awful cockpit vision.

Throughout the period in which I had been flying the German aircraft a shining silver P51D Mustang had been sitting on the tarmac and was not apparently being flown much. I had been looking forward to flying this famous fighter and the opportunity came on 18 July.

In addition to its reputation as the longest range single-engine fighter of the war, the trials reports from the Handling Squadron and Boscombe Down that we had received at Tangmere had emphasized that its general quality as a combat fighter was equal to or better than most of the enemy equipment. Some of the reports had indeed suggested overall superiority over our best fighters, but I was not sure if this was true as figures in the respective Pilot's Notes did not all support this claim. So it was with great interest that I went out to fly the 51D.

I had flown one of the first Mustang 1s to reach this country in an interesting sortie from Cranfield on 9

February 1944, and had not formed a favourable impression because of a number of drawbacks.

Its Allison engine did not have the automatic boost control which we were accustomed to in all our Merlins and Sabres so that great care was needed to avoid over-boosting, particularly during vigorous combat manoeuvres where it was most likely to occur! Additionally at that stage the Allison was under-developed and, like the Sabre in the Typhoon in 1942, was rather too prone to fail for comfort.

I had currently been testing Typhoons and Tempests at Hawker's and it was immediately apparent that this Mustang was inferior in speed and dive performance, although it had a similar rate of climb to 20,000 ft.

Its handling however was excellent and up to around 400 mph ASI its turning capability, rate of roll and gun-aiming stability all seemed comparable to the Typhoon, and better than the Spitfire V in some repsects above 350 mph.

But there the good news ended. Although I had flown Hurricanes for two years in combat, Spitfires on and off, and more recently Typhoons in test and in operations, and also a number of other fighters, I had seldom flown one with such appallingly restrictive vision!

The heavy framed windscreen arch and panel frame members, and the mixed construction canopy which seemed to consist of more metal than transparency, all added up to totally inadequate combat vision; and I was sure that it would never be accepted by the RAF for the fighter role.

For the rest, stalling and the approach and landing with its wide undercarriage giving good ground stability, were all straightforward and likely to give no problems.

In the event this model was accepted in small numbers for the army co-op reconnaissance role in which it

118

gave good service and, in particular, brought back excellent photographs of the enemy coastal defences prior to the Normandy Invasion. In parallel a heavily modified version, the Mustang III (P51B), was ordered for Fighter Command.

This type was the direct result of a valuable programme carried out by Rolls-Royce at Hucknall, who in 1943 installed a Merlin engine and revised radiator system into a Mustang I. The flight testing carried out by Ronnie Harker showed such marked improvements in performance, with potential to out-perform even the Spitfire IX and XIV in some respects, that Harker reported in the strongest terms and very effectively that it should be put into immediate production for the RAF.

In parallel, the cockpit vision problem was tackled in this country by Marcel Lobelle at White Waltham, and a much-improved 'Malcolm Lobelle' one-piece sliding canopy was introduced for the British production run by North American.

These measures, coupled with the exceptional fuel capacity of the basic Mustang provided Fighter Command with limited numbers of a capable long-range fighter for the 1944–45 period. This improved aircraft could take on a wide range of roles including air superiority, bomber escort and ground attack, and especially long-range interdiction which it did with great success led by Wing leaders Geoffrey Page, 'Birdie' Bird Wilson and Robin Johnston.

It could get as far as Berlin although, as a fighter pilot was quoted as saying at the time, 'Who the hell would want to do that?'

From this successful programme with the P51B sprang directly the massive procurement for the USAAF of the P51D with Packard Merlin, six .5-in machine-guns (replacing four in the earlier versions) and a fine one-piece

119

rear-view canopy matching the quality of the canopies on the FW-190, Tempest and later series Typhoons.

Said by many to have been 'the finest fighter of World War II', the stalwarts of the USAAF 8th Air Force flew their P51s all over Europe in 1944–45 escorting heavy bombers to Berlin and beyond; and there is no doubt that their qualities of combat handling, performance, reliability and extreme long range were a unique combination.

There were some aspects in which some of the newer Allied and enemy fighters performed better however, although none could approach the 51's range except the P47 Thunderbolt, but it could not match the 51 in combat manoeuvrability.

So it was with interested anticipation that I climbed into the cockpit of this P51D.

P51D 18 July 1945

Here again was a 'furnished' cockpit laid out like the FW-190 in a side consoles and front main panel arrangement which had clearly been purpose-designed in contrast to the rather haphazard arrangements which persisted in most British cockpits of the period with their maze of pipes, 'Jubilee' clips, add-on brackets and bent tin sub-panels in profusion.

In defence it was always said that, 'Well they worked alright, didn't they?' But it was many years after the war before cockpit ergonomics and planning for cleanliness and orderliness became an accepted function of fighter cockpit design in this country.

One notable comparison between the P51D's cockpit and the 190 was the standard blind flying panel (similar to ours) with an artificial horizon at top centre. The 190 and 109 had no artificial horizon throughout much of the war, which made their cloud penetrations more complicated than need be.

This 51D had the full rear-vision sliding canopy and slimmed-down forward windscreen members similar to our Tempests, and its combat vision was obviously excellent.

The Packard Merlin 61 rumbled characteristically into life and on the engine panel the gauges were all familiar. Taxying out immediately gave a feeling of solid security. The wide-track undercarriage was soft in action and there was little tendency to swing, although the rudder pedal-operated brakes were soft in differential steering operation and, like the German aircraft, needed close attention from a pilot more used to the British stick-lever and rudder-bar differential brake operation.

But there were no problems here, and when lined up on Tangmere's westerly runway and with Tower clearance to climb straight ahead and clear the circuit to ten miles before any manoeuvres, I set fine pitch and opened up smoothly to full boost, checked the mag. switches and released the brakes.

Acceleration was less than that of the lighter Spitfire IX or a Tempest but enough to be interesting, and the tail did not want to come up without a little forward stick. Steering the runway centre-line was easy, and then at 65–70 mph ease back the stick — airborne in virtually lever flight. Clean up undercarriage — positive and satisfying thuds and lights. Pitch and throttle to climb power at 165 and this handsome fighter immediately felt tailored to the pilot.

All aeroplanes have their own characteristics, some good, some not so good and some exceptional. As this sortie developed through performance climb and levels, and limit dives and combat manoeuvres at the high and low ends of the speed range, I could find nothing to criticize about this fine aeroplane which seemed to have all the qualities a fighter pilot could wish for.

Solid engineering, smooth responsive and powerful engine. Fine manoeuvrability all round the flight envelope with a smooth, precision feel about the all push-rod-operated flying controls. Superb cockpit vision. Fine gun-aiming stability and, most important, good control power remaining in pitch and roll at the briefed Vne, 485 mph IAS.

At the slow speed end the stall was innocuous, and from the crispness of the controls and good damping on all axes at the datum cruise speed, I could tell that this aircraft would be an excellent formation-keeper.

After an hour I had finished, but was reluctant to bring this fine fighter home for the approach and landing which were so easy and undramatic as to make a repeat unnecessary.

But when I came to write a summary report I found it difficult to complete the eulogy. The P51D was undoubtedly the most straightforward and viceless fighter of its time, and with its long range capability quite unique. But the experience had left an odd feeling — it was in fact rather too bland to be fully enjoyable in the sense that the elegant Spitfire or the thundering, crisp and operationally capable Tempest V were.

The very delicacy of Spitfires, and the manoeuvrable 545 mph Vne plus four high-velocity 20-mm Hispano cannons of the Tempest (compared to the .5-in machine-guns of the 51) were points that the 51 could not match.

So I gave my view that the P51 was still, in 1945, the best combination of fighter virtues available with a range of over 1000 miles, but that for specific operations at shorter range the later marks of Spitfire were superior above 30,000 ft, and that in all respects except for range, below 20,000 ft the Tempest was the better fighter. At that stage the Allied jets did not mount a practical challenge.

In 1990 I renewed acquaintance with this classic fighter when I flew with Delta captain Connie Bowlin in her (and husband Ed's) superb P51D at the USAF Staff College, Maxwell AFB, Alabama, and I felt that that earlier assessment still rang true. It would have been nice to have had a fighter pilot like Connie in my Tempest Wing, but it might not have been good for discipline!

Ju-88 G-1 NF. TP190. 14 and 16 July 1945

While concentrating on the single-engine fighters at Tangmere I had been aware of a large, dark and menacing shape at the Enemy Aircraft Flight dispersal on the west side of the field which I had not seen flown since I arrived. It was a Ju-88 G-1 night fighter variant, RAF serial TP190, and as 88s had always impressed us since the days in 1940 when they often dived away from our Hurricanes, I decided to investigate.

The Flight Lieutenant in charge said no, he hadn't flown it, but I could if I liked. There were the Handling Notes and, 'the Flight Sergeant can show you how to start it up.'

My only previous experience of twin-engined aircraft had been a few flights in Airspeed Oxfords and a Westland Whirlwind, which hardly qualified me for direct conversion onto a medium/heavy twin; but as no one seemed about to veto the idea I decided to try it!

But even in the casual atmosphere prevailing this seemed to be taking informality to the extreme, and I began to wonder whether it would not be better to wait until I could at least talk to a pilot who had flown one.

However this seemed to be unlikely of achievement and so on 14 July 1945 I climbed up the ladder into the high cabin of this large aeroplane, wondering if what I was about to do was really responsible or was even within the practical capabilities of a fighter-trained pilot.

In the event the Ju-88 G-1 night fighter presented no problems. The greenhouse-type construction of the cabin and nose windscreen which from outside seemed to provide a tremendous area of transparency, from inside seemed to consist almost entirely of thick metal frames. It was all sound and solid, but surprisingly restrictive in the vision sense.

The controls and instrument layout were conventional but with the advantage of electrical trimming as in the contemporary FW-190; and the only complexity seemed to be the fuel system which, designed for a bomber with multiple tanks and associated fuel cocks, clearly needed a proper degree of knowledge by the crew.

In this case with the 'crew' limited to me, I had been told to 'set the cocks on the main tanks and leave 'em there and don't stay up for more than two hours!'

This seemed like good advice, and so I started the engines under the direction of the Flight Sergeant who shouted through the open hatch below my feet.

The large paddle-bladed propellers revolved readily and sprang into smooth life with a rumble reminiscent of a vintage car, but this soon changed to a higher-pitched and aggressive noise level as power was increased. In fact this turned out to be a noisier than expected aeroplane, but that was about the only criticism. Control checks showed smooth, friction-free travel with no noticeable back-lash or 'lost motion'.

On initial taxying in the nose-high, tail-down attitude of this aircraft with its tail-wheel and tall main under-carriage, there was an awkward feeling that it could easily

124

over-swing on the turn especially downwind; but once lined up on the runway the feeling of being in a much larger aeroplane than one's previous experience had practically gone, and the 88 felt a compact and well-organized aeroplane.

Checking the mags. in a short run-up to less than full power on both caused the pedal-operated brakes to slip and produced a crescendo of sound that was impressive.

I had decided to increase to maximum power progressively on take-off to forestall any unbriefed tendency to swing, but this was not necessary and the 88 unstuck at about 70 mph at less than full throttle and without any further elevator activity after my initial action to lift the tail conventionally with forward wheel to an appropriate take-off attitude.

The initial climb was brisk, and I needed to retract the undercarriage before setting climb power in order to avoid over-stepping the under-carriage limit.

Cleaned up, the rate of climb in this light configuration was similar to a Mosquito and the aircraft responded pleasantly to the controls with light ailerons and conventional harmonization. I noticed that it needed commendably little trimming and only when levelling out at 4,000 ft and throttling back to cruise at about 230 mph* were small tweaks of the elevator and rudder trim switches required.

With time to look around, the big BMW 801 engines with their large propeller spinners reaching forward of the cockpit, and beyond them the long tapering wing tips, were a reminder that this was in fact a heavy 60-ft-span aircraft, but it was gentle and undemanding to fly in these conditions and reasonably quiet at cruising power.

---

* British standard ASI fitted for trials.

A look around over my shoulder showed that a degree of visibility existed towards the tail through the canopy structure of the top gunner's position, but that forward vision was poor and interrupted by the complex metal framework of windscreen and canopy.

Rapidly gaining confidence with this fine aeroplane I looked at partial rolls, tight turns, rolling pull-outs and dives, climbs and wing-overs; and in all of these the aircraft was stable, responsive and apparently viceless except for the noise level which reached a crescendo in dives around 300 mph IAS and was distracting. But this large aeroplane was becoming really enjoyable!

Returning towards Tangmere, I was about to slow down to look at slow speed behaviour when I noticed a Mosquito in the circuit below. Thinking it might be Bob Braham, also a member of the Tactics Branch and the leading exponent of long-range Mosquito fighter operations, I rolled down towards him and increased power; and it was immediately apparent that it was Bob and that he wanted a fight!

The Mosquito wound into the turn in my direction streaming wing tip vortices, and with full throttle and fine pitch I pulled the 88 into a vertical bank after him. The results were impressive, for although I did not know the aircraft it was easy to hold firmly on the opposite side of the circle to the Mosquito and begin to make progress towards getting on his tail.

Braham got down to work then and took the Mosquito on to its stall boundary with wings rocking perceptibly, but I could still see him in my forward arc and was not far off getting enough lead-angle for a firing position after a number of descending full power turns over Tangmere which had the station out watching. But then, rocking in his wake turbulence at only a hundred feet, I felt that discretion had to be the better

126

part of valour as I was getting into areas in which I could not possibly know the 88's characteristics, so I eased up and out of the turn and Bob Braham was promptly round on my tail.

It had been a remarkable demonstration of the handling and manoeuvring qualities of the 88 and I suddenly felt very much at home in it, but there was still the landing to come.

This interlude had used up a fair amount of main tank fuel, not to mention adrenalin, so I decided to have a brief look at handling in the landing configuration and then return to base.

Again the 88 behaved impeccably with undercarriage and flaps down and, when turning onto 'Finals' keeping the traditional 'plus 5 mph' over the Pilots' Notes figure until safely over the threshold, I found that this big aeroplane could be steered on the approach as gently and responsively as any fighter. Levelling out and closing the throttles slowly, a gentle rumble indicated that the main wheels were already on the runway, owing to slight misjudgement of height from this high cockpit while considering whether to go for a classy '3-point' landing, and so I swallowed pride and easing the wheel forward to prevent any bump-induced excursions back into the air, completed a smooth, uncomplicated and classic 'wheeler'.

This flight and another on 16 July were enough to show why the 88 series was regarded by the Germans as their best medium twin of the World War II period; and the performance of this version when matched against the latest Mosquito of 1945 was remarkable in relation to the fact that, apart from increased power and fin/rudder area in this night-fighter variant, the basic 88 airframe was largely unaltered from the 1940 bomber version.

127

It has remained in my rating as one of the best heavy piston-engined twins of all time, and a very pleasant flying experience.

Towards the end of this busy month came some light relief when a notice appeared in our office to the following effect: 'W/Cdr R.P. Beamont to No. 1 Helicopter conversion unit for course on Sikorsky R4B'.

Which humourist had caused this; Batchy Atcherley, Douglas Bader or whoever I never did discover, but as little was known at Tangmere of this very recently formed unit at Andover I was quite intrigued to find out about it.

So, on 19 July I flew over in Spitfire IX MA657 to the old World War I grass airfield which seemed to have changed little since I had force-landed my Hurricane there when lost on a dark night in 1940.

As I taxied in, by the old watch office (by now called Air Traffic Control) were two odd shapes which looked very much like large dragonflies, but they had rotary wings and small directional tail rotors.

Checking in at the unit office I met S/Ldr Basil Arkell, the CO and later to become one of the first helicopter specialist pilots in British civil aviation.

After only a brief indoctrination into the design and operational philosophy of these new-era vehicles, I went out to the aircraft with instructor F/Lt Harper.

Giving an explanation of the function of the basic controls, conventional stick for roll and pitch and rudder pedals for yaw, Harper then described the use of the cyclic pitch lever with twist-grip throttle and emphasized that the RPM must on no account be allowed to drop to the red line on the gauge as the blades could break off and allow the device to stop flying!

The engine controls and instruments were otherwise standard and the fuel system simple, and so the engine was started and the rotor RPM built up to warm-up speed.

Harper then demonstrated take-off with maximum power and progressive lift of the cyclic pitch lever until, in the hover at a few feet, he checked into wind to stop drift and then, with forward stick, pitched nose-down to accelerate away into shallow climb.

While being impressed by all this I was even more so by the high level of noise, vibration and general commotion that was going on, and wondered if we might have engine trouble. Harper said no, it was always like this and got worse at some points, and then he said, 'You've got her.'

This turned out to be an overstatement. We weaved, yawed and wallowed in the general direction of Thruxton which was the unit's training area, and there I was introduced to the mysteries of the use of cyclic pitch in the hover, descent, landing and lift-off again to hover. Unlike fixed-wing type conversions this one did not come naturally and afterwards, as I flew the elegant Spitfire IX smoothly back to Tangmere the comparison was simply no-contest.

For the next visit to Andover on 25 July I took a Spitfire XVI with the new clear-view sliding canopy, and enjoyed it. This really improved the Spit!

The CO, Basil Arkell, took this sortie on KK977 and put me through everything I had tried to learn on the first flight plus emergency procedures including simulated engine-out and auto-rotation landings. In his skilled hands it seemed simple, but the margins for achieving safe auto-rotation after sudden engine failure were, I felt, very small. He also stressed the danger of damaging the tail rotor by too much pitch angle on take-off and landing.

After an hour's strenuous work-out at Thruxton, Arkell said, 'Go back to base and land as if I wasn't here!'

and when I had achieved this he said, 'Next time you go solo.'

Again in the contrasting smooth precision of the Spitfire on the way home I wondered about the roughness, instability, general trickiness and the very small margins of performance of the R4B — it would barely take-off on a hot day with two up and full fuel!

I also wondered about the complicated control task the pilot had to perform to act as a human constant-speed unit in controlling a basically unstable vehicle. So I decided that helicopters would not be for me until they had two engines and could fly safely on one and had pilot control through an auto-pilot system, all of which of course happened in subsequent years.

I was not sure whether going back for my solo would be a good idea, but on the following day I was posted to the OATS course at Cranwell and notified that following that I was to take command of 124 Wing at Chilbolton.

This was the first Wing with the new Tempest 2s, and I was tasked with taking it out to Tiger Force in Burma against the Japanese. So I never did qualify on helicopters, and the Japanese war ended so I didn't get to Burma either — neither was a great disappointment!

So this fascinating interlude at Tangmere ended. In less than two months I had flown fourteen types including nearly all the best fighters on both sides in Europe, and this experience had left clear conclusions.

The new jet Meteor still did not amount to an effective fighter, but development in this field would surely lead to the fighters of the future.

Though high-quality fighters, the German piston-engined single seaters could not match* our Tempest below 20,000 ft or the later Spitfires or the P51 above 30,000 ft; and no one could match the P51D for long-range operations; but overall the Tempest V had come out clearly as the best of all multi-role fighters for the air war below 20,000 ft in 1944–45.

Finally, the Tempest V's vulnerable radiator system had been eliminated with the Centaurus radial of the new Tempest 2 which was also a little faster at all altitudes, and it was with this fine fighter that I was about to rejoin the operational squadrons.

After those eight months in the Stalags, things were looking up!

* Except perhaps the Ta-152 which we had not flown.

CHAPTER 8

CONCLUSION

So at Tangmere, after the end of hostilities in 1945 and with time to consider the wealth of operational experience available from all the major theatres of the air war in Europe, Russia, the Mediterranean and North Africa, Burma and the Pacific, it could be seen that the adaption of the air combat fighter, by all the air forces involved, to the specific role of pin-point ground attack had been not only an outstanding technical success but a major contribution to winning the ground battle in every campaign in which it had been employed.

It seemed inevitable that fighters of the future would now be developed with multi-role capability from the start but this was not to be, at least for some years to come.

Concurrently with the peace treaties of 1945 aviation was now entering an entirely new field — the era of the gas turbine 'jet' engine which was within a few years to more than double the performance of both military and civil aircraft.

But all of the first and most of the second generation jet fighters on both sides of the Atlantic were designed strictly as 'air-superiority fighters' with no specific ground-attack role, as it was claimed that 'modern speeds would make ground attack impossible'. A fallacy repeated decade after decade since World War 1.

Once again after some years came the realization that although the air forces of the West were equipped with efficient air superiority fighters such as the F86, Hunter and Mystere, with the phasing out of the Typhoons, Tempests, Mustangs and Thunderbolts there was, in the early 1950s, nothing in the inventory or the training syllabus of the RAF to take on the vital tactical ground-attack role in the event of hostilities.

By the mid-1950s this dangerous shortfall was becoming recognized, and the development of jet fighter types already in service to carry bomb and rocket ground-attack armament was under way again. But still no sign in the west of a dedicated tactical fighter design.

The breakthrough occurred in the late 1960s with the evolution in Europe of the international SEPECAT Jaguar fighter-bomber, an aircraft much criticised during its early service as being too dedicated to the one role (ground-attack), but which ultimately proved in the acid test of the Gulf War of 1991 to be a highly accurate and successful pin-point strike aircraft (with a nil loss record); and in America the F-111.

In parallel to this development and stemming directly from early Jaguar experience came the multi-national Panavia Tornado — a design specifically dedicated to creating the most effective low-level penetration strike fighter in the world for the NATO front line.

This design was based on the by now accepted philosophy that the only sure way of penetrating sophisticated modern defences and delivering a knock-out blow with pin-point accuracy to hardened and protected targets was with a fast, robust, manoeuvrable fighter-type aircraft sized to carry a suitable load of fuel and 'smart' weapons over an operationally significant range at, when necessary, very low altitude to stay below the enemy's defence radar vision.

134

To achieve this the very highest level of advanced technology in sensors, communications, automaticity and weapons systems was evolved, and the results were seen conclusively in the Gulf War, which was the first major conflict in history to be virtually decided in the air before the ground forces moved forwards to capture their objectives.

All the classic roles of air power were involved; air superiority fighters, heavy long-range bombers, tactical strike fighters, high and low altitude reconnaissance, fleet carrier strike aircraft, flight refuelling tankers, AWACs airborne control radars and heavy logistic transports; and strike and rescue helicopters, together with a number of innovative systems such as Stealth and Cruise Missiles were used with great effectiveness.

In all this the advanced technology of the West was revealed to maximum advantage by an exceptionally high rate of target acquisition and strike accuracy. Within the first few days a success rate with the advanced strike fighters of one weapon direct-hit per target was seen to be almost the norm, and second strikes on important targets were seldom required.

It appeared at first that the technology and training of the Allied air forces had completely outclassed the numerically superior Iraqi forces, but as the air-war progressed rapidly from the achievement of air superiority to complete air supremacy after one week of hostilities, it seemed that the total failure of the Iraqi air and ground-to-air defences against the technical and tactical superiority of the Allies was due, not only to shortcomings in their mainly Russian technology equipment, but also to Iraqi inability to deploy and operate their massive forces effectively in a modern war environment.

Be that as it may, in the short period of less than four

135

weeks the Allied air forces completely neutralized the Iraqi air and ground-to-air defences throughout the country, and so were soon able to strike at any target at will with negligible losses, virtually paralysing the enemy's communications system and enabling the Allied ground forces to move forward and take all their objectives with minimal casualties.

Loss of Iraqi life, both military and civilian, had been tragically high when the cease-fire was called to halt the carnage at a point in the campaign when the Allies had relieved Kuwait, their main objective, and were already poised to capture Basra and then take Baghdad in order to destroy the regime of Saddam Hussein. But that clearly available option created by the brilliant success of the Allied military forces was lost by political decision, and the ensuing chaos in the area of the Gulf states is, at the time of writing, no nearer to a stabilizing solution.

The successful air operation against Iraq was the result of superbly professional use of the world's most advanced technology in military aviation and demonstrated the determination, fighting fitness and superior training of all the Allied air forces involved.

But there was one outstanding feature in the air battle; the Iraq war was won primarily by the deadly accuracy of strike fighters such as the Tornado, F-16, Stealth Fighter and Jaguar.

In 1944–45 the Tempests and Typhoons had shown the way forward. An RAF Operational Research Section report of May 1945 stated:

'Nearly 60% of all the 2nd TAF loco attacks were undertaken by pilots of 122 (Tempest) Wing. At this Wing the standard of shooting is much above average'.

And in an RAF 2nd Tactical Air Force intelligence report, November 1945:

136

'the enemy-aircraft-destroyed total (by 122 Wing) was equal first with 126 (Spitfire) Wing, but the Tempest's ground (attack) scores were unapproached by any other unit'.

And now, in the 1990s, the strike fighter has become a dominant weapon in winning a major war.

APPENDICES

Station Intelligence Reports representing many hundreds of similar operations flown by 609 (WR) Typhoon Squadron in 1942–43, and by 150/122 Tempest Wing in 1944.

Appendix 1 (See p.32)

RAF Manston Intelligence Report on the first moonlight night ground attack by Typhoons.

FINAL INTRUDER REPORT — 609 SQUADRON, RAF MANSTON, KENT. NIGHT OF 17–18 NOV 1942

1 Typhoon Ib, 609 West Riding Squadron (S/L Beamont DFC) left Manston 2020 hours for Intruder Operations Berck-Abbeville-Amiens. Possible targets: trains, barges, or E/A over Amiens-Glisy aerodrome. Crossing English coast at Dungeness, he crossed Channel climbing to 8,000 ft. Weather was 10/10ths cloud at 2000 ft over Channel, extending to two miles inland, which effectually prevented opposition from S/Ls or Flak on making landfall at Berck at 6000 ft. Between this point and Abbeville, where 10/10ths cloud and fog began, weather was clear moonlight except for ground haze. After proceeding at 3000 ft via Somme estuary along the

Somme-Abbeville canal, where no activity was seen, S/L Beamont turned and found a train proceeding towards coast between Port-le-Grand and Doyelles-sur-Mer, and consisting mainly of box-like coaches. He made five right-angle attacks opening fire at 500/1000 ft and firing an average burst of 2½–3 secs. After the second attack the train halted and the locomotive was enveloped in steam. From the middle of the train intermittent dull-red explosions were seen both during and after attack. On breaking away from the first two attacks, S/L Beamont passed over St Valerie-sur-Somme where a searchlight illuminated him and held him for 0–2,500 ft despite evasive action, to the accompaniment of accurate fire from 4 Bofors guns in the same position. During subsequent attacks this position was avoided. After the last attack S/L Beamont re-crossed coast at Berck at 5000 ft and landed at Manston at 2125. Time over target: 2045–2105.

Points of Interest

1 Plotting lights which followed, but were not necessarily beneath.

2 A semi-obscured winking orange glow seen from inland, apparently on a hill near Lancheres.

3 A yellow searchlight in Boulogne area, with red self-destroying tracer going up beam and bursting yellow.

4 Three bomb bursts between Boulogne and Calais.

5 Slight difficulty was experienced during initial stages of each attack in getting sight on to target owing to ground haze and narrow vertical angle of vision of Typhoon aircraft.

Sgd. F H ZEIGLER, Flying Officer
Intelligence Officer, No 609 WR Squadron

Distribution:
Station Commander, Biggin Hill
Station Commander, Manston
W/C Gleed, H.Q.F.C.
W/C Walker, HQ No 11 Group
Senior Controller, 'Intruder' Ops

Appendix 2 *(See page 32)*

FINAL INTRUDER REPORT

609 WEST RIDING SQUADRON, RAF MANSTON,
21–22 NOVEMBER 1942

1 Typhoon Ib (S/Ldr Beamont DFC) t/o Manston 2155
for intruder to Abbeville-Amiens area and to attack
trains. Crossed coast over Le Touquet at 2128 at 7000 ft
diving through small break in cloud about 10 miles inland. On way to Abbeville saw train between Le Crotoy
and Noyelles but did not attack. At 2140 near Conde-
Folie a second train of goods wagons was attacked,
strikes being seen along the wagons. Patrol continued
towards Amiens, where blackout was noted to be very
bad, many windows being left uncurtained. No activity
at Glisy so returned to Abbeville, seeing a train near
Hangest-sur-Somme, with engine emitting steam, but on
approach of Intruder train shut off steam and was lost.
Arrived over Abbeville area as 2210, flying at 300 ft with
navigation lights on and reconnoitred Drucat but saw
no activity or aircraft. On crossing marshalling yards
had noticed a long stationary train to which Intruder

returned and attacked from 50 ft, engine emitting much steam. Returned and made second attack from same height, when engine tender burst into flames and engine disappeared in clouds of smoke and steam which could be seen in an ascending column 250 ft high from Le Crotoy. A second engine was also hit and emitted much steam and 4 lines of goods wagons were also attacked, using up all cannon observing strikes on all rows. By this time about 10 Bofors had opened up at low angle from NE of Abbeville, so returned home, crossing out over Hardelot at 5000 ft at 2220 landing at base at 2230.

Weather: Cloud base at coast 2500 ft, top 7000 ft, 10/10ths. Inland base 2000 top 3000 9/10. Visibility — moderate.

Note: S/L Beamont found that light of bursting cannon shells on lines was very useful in illuminating target and was able to correct his aim. He also notes that low-level attack of this type makes trains stand out very well against the landscape.

Second sortie:

1 Typhoon Ib (S/Ldr Beamont DFC) t/o Manston 0013 for anti-train operations in Lille area. Crossed coast over Mardyck at 0023 at 8000 ft diving to 900. At 0028 saw a stationary train, very long heading N composed of low flat trucks, believed to be an ammunition train. Attacked twice, each time receiving Bofors fire from truck immediately behind engine tender. Strikes were seen on the trucks, attacks being made from 100–80 ft. Weather conditions further inland made attempt to reach Lille impossible, so turned SW and flew to Le Touquet via Hazebrouck and St Omer. At Le Touquet asked for a vector and crossed coast at approx 0048 at 10,000 ft landing at Manston at 0100 hrs. While in vicinity of St Omer saw what appeared to be a house

on fire. No S/Ls or flak (other than from the train).
Weather: 20 miles off coast 4/10 cloud base 2000 increasing to 10/10 top at 7000. Inland 10/10 top 10,000 descending to 300 in sleet showers, icing throughout. Area Mardyck-Hazebrouck-Oostende slightly clearer.
Note: S/L Beamont is certain that the fire from train was Bofors and not Oerlikon, bursts being seen at approx 8000 ft being red in colour. Fire was not opened up until Intruder had just passed over, ie, from immediately behind.

R C TREWEEKS, P/O
For Station Intelligence Officer.
RAF Station, Manston, Kent.

Appendix 3 *(See p.32-34)*

RAF Manston 11 Group Fighter Command Combat Report (The first daylight ground-attack sortie by 609 Squadron Typhoons)

To: HQ 11 Group (R) Hornchurch
From: Manston

MI/7 13/12 COMPOSITE RHUBARB REPORT 13/12/42 (A) 609 (B) 2 Typhoons (C) 1449–1545 (D) Amiens-Abbeville Rly, Glisy A/D (E) 15 minutes (F) 3 locomotives Cat B and rolling stock damaged (G) Nil
GENERAL: 5 bursts 'friendly' medium ack-ack 100 yd behind on crossing coast out to sea at 800 ft between Folkestone and Dungeness. Made landfall Cayeux 1502 hrs at 6000 ft cloud 10/10 at 5/6000 ft, higher inland, with some showers, vis 30/40 miles. Flew at 5000 ft to

143

W of Abbeville, reconnoitred Drucat A/D from W, nothing seen. S/L Beamont attacked train with large engine, 10 open and 2 closed trucks ahead W on Abbeville-Le Tréport line at 660826 (sheet 9D/4). Fired 4-second burst in dive from 1600–100 ft. Strikes observed on trucks, then on engine, which stopped with bright flash and erupting steam. F/O Lallemand (Belgian) also fired short burst, but did not press home attack as train already immobilised. S/L Beamont then returned, cockpit door having opened in dive. F/O Lallemand continued W, and between 2 reservoirs at Ancheville (540758 sheet 9D/6) attacked engine and tender. Fired several short bursts from 1000–50 ft, saw strikes and steam. Proceeding W, F/O Lallemand saw goods train going S between Greny and Auquemesnil (400690 sheet 9D/5). Fired short bursts at 1000 and 50 ft, saw 5 strikes second burst, but shooting difficult owing stoppages on 3 cannons. Saw personnel on believed Derchigny a/d running for blister hangars, and experienced light flak thence. Looking back saw steam from last engine attacked. Recrossed coast on Berneval at 3000 ft. Films exposed by both pilots — 1720A.

Station Intelligence Officer
RAF Manston

Appendix 4 (See p.32-34)

TO: H.Q. 11 GROUP. (R) HORNCHURCH

FROM: MANSTON

M1/2 18/4 COMPOSITE AND FINAL INTRUDER REPORT 18/4/43

144

(A) 609 (B) TYPHOON 1B (S/LDR BEAMONT) (C) 0115–0216 (D) RAILWAYS GRIS NEZ — DIEPPE (E) N/A (F) 2 LOCOS CAT.D ROLLING STOCK FIRED AND DAMAGED. (G) NIL. GENERAL.

In at Cap Gris Nez, out Boulogne. Attacked as follows. Utilising Marker-Beacon found train in cutting W. of Phien-Le-Guines. Strikes seen on engine (steam emitted) and on rolling stock. On breaking away Oerlikon vertical fire from train. Second short attack no results observed. This engine completes 609 Squadron's one hundredth damaged engine since December. At Rang-du-Flier train attacked just south of station. Strikes all along train but no other results observed. 5 rounds of 20 mm from Pt. Marais. At Rue long passenger train seen going north at full speed. Attacked at Langreville. And strikes seen all along train and engine which stopped enveloped in steam. Two more attacks made. At Noyelles-Sur-Mer line of goods trucks in station. Attacked and one left emitting red flames. Proceeded to Abbeville-Amiens but no activity. Returned, saw truck still burning and attacked engine at Langreville again. This time 4 × 20 mm guns put up a barrage. Guns appear to have been mobile as came from sides of track and had not fired on first attack. First and second engines sighted through fire-box doors being open. Three searchlights south east of Boulogne followed aircraft's path. Weather visibility very good. Slight ground haze. No further report 18/0408B.

Station Intelligence Officer
RAF Manston

Appendix 5 *(See p.32-34)*

FINAL INTRUDER REPORT — 609 SQUADRON

17 — 18/1/43

Six patrols by Typhoon 1B were flown over France and Belgium, one pilot making two sorties. The night's total claims were:

S/Ldr Beamont DFC:3 locomotives Cat B

Rolling stock damaged

3 lorries damaged

F/Lt de Selys (Belgian): 1 locomotive Cat B

F/O van Lierde (Belgian): 1 locomotive Cat B

S/Ldr Beamont (2019-2135) set out to patrol the Lille-Douai area. He crossed in at Calais/Gravelines at 5000 feet and flew to Merville where he saw the aerodrome lit as he approached but as he arrived the lights were doused. He orbited, flashing 'Q' on his downward recognition light and the A/D lit up again, the lighting consisting of the N.E. arm of the V/L and crossbars, and W A/D boundary lights. These doused as S/Ldr Beamont crossed the A/D. White Very lights were fired.

He proceeded to Valenciennes where a long line of white lights (V/L) was observed running N.E. to S.W. across a wood north of the town. The A/D (Denain/Prouvy) was not lit, although a few red obstruction lights were seen in the vicinity. Beacon S.E. of town, 2 white lights flashing alternately.

S/Ldr Beamont then went to Lille where Lille/Nord was on. Here again the lights (6 white leading-in lights and red boundary lights) doused but came on again when 'Q' was flashed on the D.R.L. S/Ldr Beamont noticed that many factory chimneys, gasometers and high buildings in the northern outskirts of Lille bore red obstruction lights. A series of white and green Very

146

lights were fired from the A/D when he headed away.

The pilot next returned to Merville where he once more obtained a display of lights (as before) by flashing the magic letter 'Q'. He turned away west and saw, 5 miles west of the A/D, a white V (about 5 lights in each arm) pointing towards the A/D, flashing on and off. 1 S/L from Merville A/D failed to illuminate, and 1 Bofors fired a few rounds.

He turned N.W. and when just south of Calais saw a long goods train consisting of open trucks (apparently laden) and box wagons, stationary on an embankment at Folio B, Sheet 2, Ref. 839708. He attacked this seeing his shells burst near the engine, and the train began to move forward towards a cutting a little further south. Making a second attack the pilot saw strikes on the engine, which stopped in a cloud of steam. He made three of four more attacks, raking the whole length of the train until his ammunition was exhausted. He recrossed the coast between Calais and Gris Nez diving from 5000 feet, and returned direct to base. Many S/Ls were seen at Calais.

F/Lt de Selys (Belgian) (2013–2148) flew to the N.W. outskirts of Brussels, crossing the coast at East of Dunkirk at 8000 feet evading a cone of 13 S/Ls by diving. The outward journey was uneventful, and it was not until the pilot reached the Ghent-Courtrai railway on the direct route home that he found a target. Here, at a point about 5 miles S.W. of Deynze, he saw a goods train moving S.W. He attacked this from N.W. to S.E. seeing strikes on the engine, and it stopped. Turning, he made a second attack from N. to S. and saw his fire apparently hitting just behind the engine. As he was about to pass over the front of the train there was a vivid yellowish-white flash and the pilot felt his aircraft thrown upwards by the force of the explosion. Turning back he saw burning debris scattered round the front of the train. During this second attack Bofors and machine-gun fire was experienced from West and South of the train.

F/Lt de Selys recrossed coast east of Dunkirk (only 1 S/L) returning direct to base. Flares were seen West of Brussels on both journeys. On outward journey red and white beacon seen at Gris Nez also S/L pointing inland and alternating between vertical and horizontal positions. Powerful flashing light in Nivelles area.

F/O Raw (2050–2150) chose railways south of Le Tréport and Dieppe as his objective. Approaching the French coast north of Cayeux at 8000 feet, when still about 5 miles out to sea, he saw a number of yellow lights appear at approximately his height, 2 or 3 either side, some distance away; these seemed to remain stationary for several seconds and were still alight when F/O Raw started to dive over the coast at Cayeux. Flattening out at 1000 feet he flew down the Le Tréport – Paris line to a point just North of Aumale and then turned West intending to pick up the Dieppe – Paris line. As he turned he saw approaching rapidly from the starboard bow two white lights, which proved to be on the wing tips of a Ju-88 which passed less than 100 feet beneath the Typhoon, then at 1500 feet. This was at approximately 2123 hours. F/O Raw turned to chase the E/A but did not see it again. He returned along the route which he had followed on the way in but found no targets to attack.

S/Ldr Beamont (2225–2345) making his second sortie, was scrambled to investigate possible enemy activity at Chievres. He crossed the coast at Gravelines at 4000 feet and after pin-pointing himself by the beacon South of Valenciennes (2 alternate rotating lights) he found the town of Mons and flew up the railway towards Ath and then picked out Chievres A/D at about

2250 hours. There was no apparent activity and after orbiting until 2300 S/Ldr Beamont returned to Mons and found a stationary goods train at Jemannes, just West of Mons. He fired a longish burst seeing strikes on the front trucks, near the engine, which may also have been hit. Observation of results was made difficult and further attacks were prevented by S/Ls and considerable light flak from the direction of Mons. The pilot set course for Lille and flew across Lille/Vendeville at 1000 feet and was picked up by S/Ls which he evaded by diving away. He saw a train at Loos (South of Lille) but the S/Ls were still pestering him so that he did not attack this; nor did he fire, for the same reason, at two other trains seen between Lille and Roubaix, further accurate S/Ls at Flers proving troublesome. Passing over Lille/Nord he ran into more S/Ls augmented by Bofors guns firing up each beam and considerable 20 mm fire.

Deciding that this area was lacking in futurity, S/Ldr Beamont went to Wevelghem where he attacked a stationary locomotive, seeing strikes and an eruption of steam. More S/Ls and co-operative light flak were experienced and in evading them S/Ldr Beamont turned across Moorseele A/D where the reception was again warm, not less than 4 S/Ls and 6 light flak posts.

Having evaded these at last, the pilot set course for home. About 5 miles south of Furnes he saw a line of lights which on closer investigation proved to be the headlights of a mile-long convoy of vehicles, apparently led by three or four motor-cycles, proceeding South. He dived to tree-top height and raked the convoy from front to rear with cannon fire. The leading vehicles, including the motor vehicles, turned abruptly off the road and hits were seen on at least 3 lorries. He came round again to repeat the attack but all the lights had been turned off and the pilot could not see the target from a sufficient distance to enable him to attack. He next moved on to a spot where he had attacked a train on the previous patrol, searchlights from Coxyde and Dunkirk exposing along his track but behind. Arriving South of Calais he found two trains converging on the scene of his first sortie attack, a passenger train from the north, at Folio B, Sheet 2, ref. 847743, and a goods train from the South at Folio B, Sheet 2, ref. 825693. This was at about 2330 hours. He fired a burst from the rear of the passenger train seeing strikes all the way along it and a shower of sparks from the middle coaches. This train shut off its steam and was lost to view, so S/Ldr Beamont went on and made a head-on attack on the goods train, seeing strikes on the engine which was at once enveloped in steam. This final burst exhausted the Typhoon's ammunition and the pilot returned to base, crossing the coast out at Calais/Gris Nez at 4000 feet.

F/O van Lierde (Belgian) (0030 Manston-0156 Bradwell Bay) crossed coast at Dunkirk at 8000 feet, noticing S/Ls between there and Ostend. He proceeded to Chievres A/D, where flare-path and obstruction lights doused as he arrived. He flashed letter 'G' without response, at Lille/Vendeville a flare path was also on. He followed the railway Lille – Orchies or Lille – Douai at about 0115 and attacked the locomotive of a goods train travelling S.W. 5 miles South of Lille. He made 3 attacks, seeing strikes on second and third, after which train stopped with much steam. Some S/Ls in Lille area failed to illuminate the Typhoon. He crossed coast East of Dunkirk. No flak experienced throughout.

F/O Evans (Canadian) (0050 Manston-0200 Bradwell Bay) crossed coast east of Calais at 5000 feet, and proceeded to Lille area, where S/Ls exposed without illuminating and fairly accurate light flak was experienced. Douai and Arras area was also patrolled without incident. Coast recrossed at Berck-sur-Mer, many red and white lights being seen from A/D from seawards. On landing at Bradwell Bay, Typhoon hit mud on edge of runway and turned on its nose. Pilot uninjured.

Weather: Generally 8/ to 10/10ths medium cloud at 8000 feet. Visibility good, but too dark for close observation of ground detail in places.

Station Intelligence Officer
RAF Manston

Appendix 6 *(See p.36)*

The Form 'D' operations order which led to the shipping strike reported in Appendix 7

FORM 'D' UE 3 IMMEDIATE SECRET NOT WT
TO HEADQUARTERS 11 GROUP RPT MANSTON
FROM HORNCHURCH
184/4/43

DRAFT CIRCUS NO (NO 5 HORNCHURCH STYLE)

1. *INFORMATION*
12 WHIRLIBOMBERS ARE CARRYING OUT AN ATTACK ON RAILWAY SIDINGS AT EU, ESCORTED BY ONE SQUADRON OF SPITFIRES VB COVER FOR WHIRLIBOMBERS IS BEING PROVIDED BY 2 SPITFIRE IX SQUADRONS
(A) ONE TYPHOON SQUADRON WILL AFFORD REAR COVER. SWEEP BEHIND BOMBERS AND ESCORT. TO SMACK DOWN ANY HUNS JUST TAKING OFF. FORMATION WILL FLY, MAKING LANDFALL OVER CAYEUX, TO MAKE HUN BELIEVE TARGET IS ABBEVILLE.

2. *EXECUTION*
ZERO (TO BE DECIDED BY 11 GROUP)

1. *TARGET*
RAILWAY SIDINGS EAST OF EU. FOR 12 WHIRLI-
BOMBERS OF 137 SQUADRON. BOMBING HEIGHT
13/7000 FT.

2. *ESCORT*
19 SQUADRON (SPITFIRE VB)

3. *ESCORT COVER AND FREE LANCE WING*
2 SPITFIRE IX SQUADRONS, 122 AND 453

4. *REAR COVER*
609 TYPHOON SQUADRON

3. *RENDEZVOUS*
HASTINGS BELOW 500 FT AT ZERO
4. *ROUTE AND TIMING*
HASTINGS ZERO. CAYEUX ZERO PLUS 19. TARGET
ZERO PLUS 23 AND OUT AT AULT.

NOTE
BOMBERS AND ESCORT WILL PROCEED AT SEA
LEVEL FOR THE FIRST 6 MINUTES THEN CLIMB
TOWARDS CAYEUX, CROSSING THE COAST AT
ZERO PLUS 19 AT 12,000 FT. TOP COVER ABOVE
BLOWER HEIGHT. THEY WILL FLY SOUTH TO RIVER
BRESLE, TURN RIGHT AND BOMB ON TURN FROM
S.E. TO N.W. DIVING FROM 13,000 TO 7,000 FT.
WITHDRAWAL WILL BE MADE OUT OVER AULT AND
AFTER CROSSING OUT BOMBERS AND ESCORT
WILL FLY AT SEA LEVEL, MAKING RETURN LAND-
FALL OVER DUNGENESS ABOVE 1,000 FT. SPITFIRE
IX SQUADRONS, IF BOMBER PARTY IS NOT
MOLESTED, WILL CLIMB FROM TARGET TOWARDS
ABBEVILLE UNDER APPLEDORE CONTROL.

5. *REAR COVER 609 TYPHOON SQUADRON.*
RENDEZVOUS HASTINGS BELOW 500 FT ZERO
PLUS 10. CAYEUX ZERO PLUS 24 AT 15/18,000 FT.
TYPHOONS WILL SWEEP BEHIND BOMBERS AND
FOLLOW THEM OUT.

SIGNALS ORGANIZATION
ALL AIRCRAFT ON HORNCHURCH SECTOR OPS
FREQUENCY = 181000

Appendix 7 *(See p.36)*

RAF Manston No 11 Group Fighter Command
Intelligence Reports

TO: HQ 11 Group Hornchurch-Swingate-VA Dover
FROM: Manston
M1/10 4/4/43 COMPOSITE RAMROD 46 REPORT
4/4/43
(A) 137 SQDN and 609 SQDN (B) 8 WHIRLIBOMBERS*
and 9 TYPHOONS 1B (C) 1816/1940 (D) ABBEVILLE
MARSHALLING YARDS (E) 1855 hrs (F) ONE FLAK
SHIP CAT 11 SHARED BY F/LT WELLS AND F/O EVANS
AND ONE R-BOAT CAT 11 AND ONE R-BOAT CAT III
SHARED BY S/LDR BEAMONT, ADJ PILOT BLANCO
(BELGIAN), F/O RAW, F/O CAMERON AND F/O VAN
LIERDE (BELGIAN) (G) ONE TYPHOON CAT B PILOT
UNINJURED

GENERAL
The Manston formations rendezvoused with 2 Spit
Sqds from Hornchurch at Hastings at 500 ft at 1830 hrs.
French coast crossed at Cayeux, Whirlibombers 8,500

---

* Westland Whirlwind twin-engined fighter bombers.

ft Typhoons 8,000 ft behind. Target bombed diving from 12,500 to 7,000 ft, 16 × 600 lbs: inst GP 4 bombs seen to burst centre of target and one on large building to the left. Other unobserved.

Formation recrossed French coast Cayeux 7,000 ft and bombers returned escorted by 2 Typhoons after No 609 Sqdn when half way over channel were vectored by Swingate direct to special target (controller P/O Manning). 6 R-boats seen in pairs, line astern towing paravanes travelling in towards Boulogne 4 miles off coast. Inshore of last pair one believed small motor flak ship. Pilots report R-boats appeared to have more than normal complement aboard. S/Ldr Beamont manoeuvred Sqdn attack down sun. All a/c made one attack each on last pair of R-boats or flak ship. Boats appeared to be taken by surprise and only opened intense return fire especially from flak ship after attack commenced. One Typhoon hit in rudder and one in engine. Flak ship and R-boat seen on fire and strikes on other R-boat. S/Ldr Beamont saw a large object fall off R-boat during his attack. Bandits reported by Hornchurch so leader ordered Squadron home landing just after Whirlibombers. During attack leading R-boats made for Boulogne. Heavy flak accurate for height out to port on entering from position 1 mile S of St Valery-sur-Somme. Over (bombing) target light flak at 5,000 ft, some heavy fairly accurate during attack. Weather, no cloud visibility 25 miles. Cine camera guns exposed. Ammo expired 2,450 rds HELAF and SAF 1.

Station Intelligence Officer
RAF Manston

Appendix 8 *(See p.60)*

RAF Newchurch No 150 Wing 11 Group Fighter Command

Combat Report.
PILOTS: W/C R BEAMONT DSO DFC & Bar P/O SLADE-
      BETTS, F/S McKERRAS, F/S FOSTER, F/S DO-
      MANSKI (POLISH) 150 Wing 28 May 1944

At 16.55 hours nine Tempests V of 3 Sqdn took off for CORMEILLE-EN-VEXIN Airfield, as information had been received that FW-190s and Me-410s were seen on a P.R.U. sortie that morning. Owing to a variety of technical troubles 4 of the Tempests came back before reaching the French coast. The remaining pilots closed-up to loose formation with W/C Beamont leading, a section to port, P/O Slade-Betts and F/Sgt McKerras, and a section to starboard, F/Sgt Foster and F/Sgt Domanski.

They crossed in at AULT at 8,000 ft and went straight to CORMEILLE-EN-VEXIN passing to the right of the airfield. In Bays on the east side of the south dispersal five T/E aircraft were seen, so W/C Beamont led the formation into a diving turn out of the sun, opening fire at about 470 ASI, range about 700 yd. The W/C's attack was from ¾ head on and his target and those of the other two sections were identified as Ju-88s, possibly Ju-188s, painted black all over. In the turn and dive P/O Slade-Betts and F/Sgt McKerras had pulled over to starboard but got into position and P/O Slade-Betts took the aircraft in the bay on the right of the W/C's target, and F/Sgt McKerras took the next on the right, both observing strikes.

F/Sgt Foster came down behind W/C Beamont, but as his windshield was oiled up he could not select a target and fired a very short burst at the same target as the leader. F/Sgt Domanski came down last, and picking the next aircraft on the right not previously attacked, gave it a burst, observing strikes.

As W/C Beamont pulled away he saw a piece of his

target fly off and the aircraft burning, and F/Sgt Domanski saw this and another target burning. As he crossed the E dispersal, F/Sgt McKerras gave a burst at some huts and saw strikes.

It was only as the section was at the intersection of the runway that inaccurate fire was opened by light guns. The formation stayed low down for 2 or 3 miles and then climbed. Smoke from two fires was seen from the target up to a distance of six miles. The formation passed BEAUVAIS Airfield where no aircraft were seen, but there were many unfilled bomb craters and damaged hangars. They crossed out at AULT at 8,000 ft landing at base at 1805 hrs.

Station Intelligence Officer
RAF Newchurch

Appendix 9 (See p.68)

RAF NEWCHURCH COMBAT REPORT. 150 WING. W/CDR R P BEAMONT DSO DFC. PILOT. 8 June 1944.

I was leading the Newchurch Tempest Wing on a fighter sweep on the Caen area of the beachhead via Rouen, Bernay and Argentan. We took off from Newchurch at 12.25 hours, and crossed the French coast at Pte d'Ailly at 10,000 ft. When we were a few miles to the West of Rouen at 12.50 hours over scattered cloud, I saw five aircraft in line astern at about 6,000 ft, turning from East to North. Leaving 486 (N.Z.) Squadron up above as top cover, I took No 3 Squadron down to investigate.

I closed in behind the aircraft at 470 IAS and

recognised them as Me-109Gs. They were travelling at approximately 300 mph and did not realise they were being bounced until just before I had opened fire, when the e/a broke to port and dived for cloud with violent evasive action. I selected the fourth or last e/a, I am not sure which, and opened fire with a 2/3 second burst, starting with 30° deflection, and changing according to the e/a's evasive action.

I opened fire at about 500 yards range closing to point blank, and saw strikes at the end of the burst on the starboard side of the fuselage. The e/a immediately poured smoke and flames. I had to break to starboard in order to avoid collision and then to port when I saw clearly the e/a enveloped in flames in an inverted dive. I broke to starboard as I finished my attack and heard a loud bang and saw a strike on my starboard wing. My No 2 who subsequently saw my e/a disintegrate and the starboard wing break off, saw two Me-109s diving down out of sun at him and myself. My u/c warning lights went on so I handed over to S/Ldr Dredge of No 3 Squadron, and set course for base where I landed at 13.30 hours.

The aircraft I destroyed was camouflaged mottled chocolate and brown and no national markings were visible.

I claim one Me-109G destroyed.

Rounds fired: 60 rounds 20 mm each gun HE1 and SAP1.

No stoppages.

Station Intelligence Officer
RAF Newchurch

Appendix 10 (See p.95-97)

FROM 56 SQUADRON OPERATIONAL DIARY 1944

Monday 2nd October VOLKEL
The squadron flew three patrols (Arnhem area). The first, led by S/Ldr Cotes Preedy was uneventful. W/Cdr Beamont led the second and 56 gained reflected glory as the W/Cdr Flying destroyed one FW-190. This was a particularly fine piece of work as the flying was done, not in the horizontal but in the vertical plane, and the W/Cdr opened fire at 510 IAS . . .

RAF VOLKEL (HOLLAND) NO 122 WING 2ND TACTICAL AIR FORCE INTELLIGENCE BULLETIN

Tuesday 3rd October 1944
Since the bulletin last appeared the Tempests have got thoroughly into their giant stride, having already destroyed 5 enemy aircraft, probably destroyed 2 and damaged 1 (since arriving in 2nd TAF on 24th September) ...

On Sept 29th 96 sorties were flown for 118 hrs flying with 3 FW-190s destroyed, 2 probables and 1 damaged, and one Tempest lost (F/O Clapperton missing) ...

On Sept 30, 71 sorties produced 110 hrs flying with 1 Me-109 destroyed and F/O Rothwell (3 Sqdn) forcelanded, unhurt.

On Oct 1st, the squadrons ... waited at Grimbergen until the mists lifted sufficiently to enable them to fly North (to Volkel). W/O Reid was shot down by flak on the way.

Oct 2nd, 74 sorties flown totalling 79 hours. Patrols of the Arnhem area uneventful except for the destruction of the Wing's 98th Hun since D-Day, a Fw-190 destroyed by W/Cdr Beamont.

Appendix 11 *(See p.94)*

Extract from a letter from A.M.F. Finucane, a platoon commander in the British Army in the battle for Germany in 1944, referring to operations of the Volkel Tempest Wing:

". . . On that Sunday (24 Sept. 1944) a week after the Arnhem landing my battalion, 7th Green Howards, were defending the south end of the big Nijmegen bridge from a threatened attack from the east. My platoon was 'dug in' on the roundabout at the city end of the bridge approach and on the receiving end of sporadic shelling. We had received warning orders to cross the bridge in mid afternoon and establish ourselves before nightfall near Bemmel village on the embankment of the (then) uncompleted highway from Nijmegen to Arnhem.

At intervals during the morning, several 'finger fours' of Tempests appeared weaving slowly under high cloud over the battle area between Nijmegen and Arnhem to the north. It was an impressive and reassuring sight. I recall my lads talking about it and commenting on the excellent air cover we had received all the way from Normandy and how 'thanks to the Tiffies and Tempests' we had never been attacked by German aircraft . . ."

BIBLIOGRAPHY

Aeroplane Monthly (IPC Magazines Ltd)

Author's RAF Pilot's Flying Log Books and Diaries, 1943, 1944, 1945.

Intelligence Reports, No. 150 Wing to No. 11 Group Fighter Command, and No. 122 Wing to No. 85 Group 2nd TAF, 1944.

Intelligence Report, 122 Wing 2nd TAF, November 1945.

Lerche, H.W., *Luftwaffe Test Pilot* (Janes).

Mason, F., *Typhoon and Tempest* (Aston Publications).

RAF Operational Research Section Report, May 1945.

Thomas, C. and Shores, C., *Typhoon and Tempest Story* (Arms and Armour Press).

INDEX